hotels • restaurants • spas • shops

beijingchic

hotels • restaurants • spas • shops

beijingchic

text paul mooney • zoë jaques • annette tan

·K·U·P·E·R·A·R·D·

executive editor
melisa teo

assistant editors
michelle low • suzanne wong

designer
lisa damayanti

production manager
sin kam cheong

first published in 2008 by
editions didier millet pte ltd
121 telok ayer street, #03-01
singapore 068590
email: edm@edmbooks.com.sg
website: www.edmbooks.com

first published in great britain 2008 by
kuperard
59 hutton grove, london n12 8ds
telephone : +44 (0) 20 8446 2440
facsimile : +44 (0) 20 8446 2441
enquiries : sales@kuperard.co.uk
website : www.kuperard.co.uk

Kuperard is an imprint of Bravo Ltd.

©2008 editions didier millet pte ltd

Printed in Singapore

isbn: 978-1-85733-418-0

COVER CAPTIONS:

1: *Room with a view at Park Hyatt Beijing.*
2: *The Peninsula Beijing's acclaimed JING.*
3: *A large incense coil at Dongyue Temple.*
4: *Devotees at the Lama Temple.*
5: *Wares on sale at Panjiayuan Market.*
6: *Surrealistic interior of Lan.*
7: *A tower overlooking Kunming Lake.*
8: *A traditional Peking opera performance.*
9: *A hawker at Panjiayuan Market takes five.*
10: *The eye-catching Tsinghua Science Park.*
11: *A model strikes a pose on the catwalk.*
12: *An elegant setting at House by the Park.*
13: *Quirky touches define GREEN T. HOUSE.*
14: *Balloons depicting Peking opera masks.*
15: *The Gate of Heavenly Peace by night.*
16: *Rechenberg's exclusive collection.*
17: *The National Stadium's striking design.*
18: *Young gymnasts in training.*
19: *GREEN T. HOUSE's sleek furnishings.*
20: *Play of natural light at GREEN T. HOUSE.*
21: *Stunning views at Bayhood No. 9.*

PAGE 2: *The Forbidden City in winter.*

THIS PAGE: *Skating lessons are a popular activity among Beijing children.*

OPPOSITE: *Stilt walkers at a festival.*

PAGE 6: *Carving on the Forbidden City wall.*

PAGE 8 AND 9: *Red lanterns along Ghost Street.*

contents

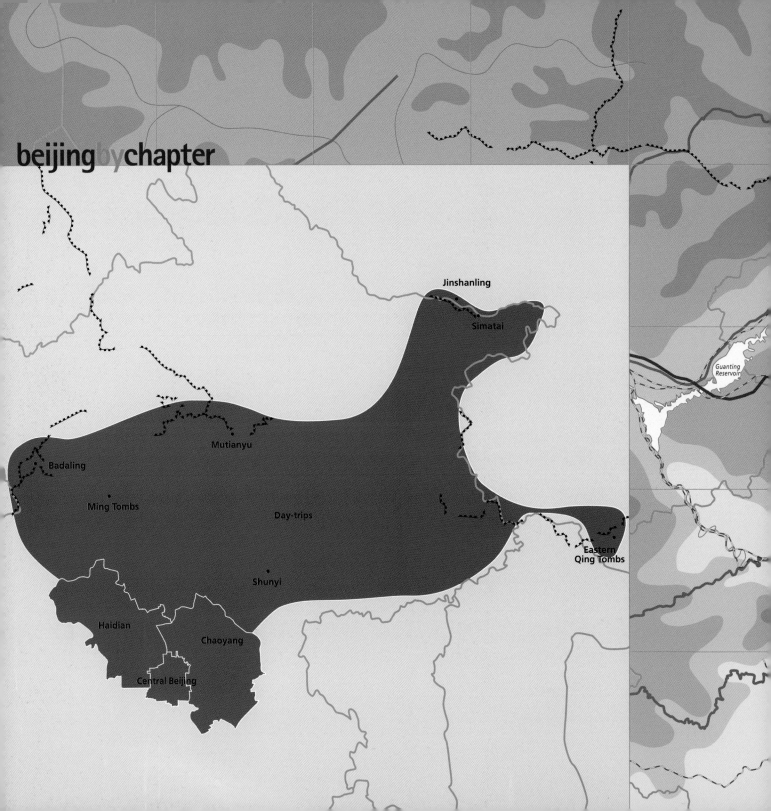

beijingbychapter

Jinshanling

Simatai

Mutianyu

Badaling

Ming Tombs

Day-trips

Shunyi

Eastern
Qing Tombs

Haidian

Chaoyang

Central Beijing

Guanting
Reservoir

beijing+surroundings

Jinshanling

Simatai

Miyun
Reservoir

Mutianyu

• Miyun

Badaling

• Ming Tombs

• Huairou

Shunyi

• Pinggu

• Eastern
Qing Tombs

Beijing

N

Legend

▬▬	Expressway
▬▬	National road
▭	Urban ring road
┼┼┼	Railway
▭	Railway station
▪▪▪	Great Wall
◠	River
◯	Lake
✈	Airport

0 km   7.5   15   22.5   30 km

introduction

the face of beijing

Many foreigners tend to think of cosmopolitan Shanghai and its energetic people as the future of China. But anyone who has spent even a little bit of time in the Chinese capital will realise that dusty and at times dowdy Beijing is the place to make it or break it. People from all over the country flock here, lured by its opportunities, the feel of cultural ferment, and the chance to reinvent themselves. Students, entrepreneurs, artists, chefs, designers and more all move around the city in a constant buzz.

While others may also think that Beijing, as the centre of the government, would be a somewhat suffocating place, Beijing's native sons and daughters have a chutzpah that makes the city famous. There is an unusual freedom here that has made the city the creative centre of China, and which attracts artists from all over. Art galleries have blossomed in hotels, courtyard houses, old factories and an ancient watchtower. This is where the recording industry is located, and where serious musicians eventually end up. There are at least twice as many bands as any other city in China, and a slew of underground clubs and booming nightspots offering live music.

Meanwhile, even entrepreneurs find Beijing a mecca because they say the risks—and rewards—are greater here. Beijing boasts the best-educated citizenry anywhere in China, producing some 80 per cent of the country's PhDs; in fact, the city's Haidian district is also known as China's Silicon Valley.

Finally, Beijing is also home to several million migrant workers, who are often referred to disparagingly as waidiren, or outsiders. This hardworking group is sometimes blamed for the problems confronting the city. However, economists say that Beijing would not be what it is today without this army of tireless labourers, construction workers, waiters and maids, who have kept the city buzzing along, taking on the kinds of jobs most others would prefer to avoid.

THIS PAGE (FROM TOP): A performer takes a break from her rehearsal, a giant Peking opera mask in the background; from dawn to dusk, a constant buzz pervades the capital.

OPPOSITE: The yellow roof tiles of the Forbidden City. In the past, only the imperial family were allowed to use this royal colour.

beginnings

For the past 3,000 years, several towns and cities of varying size and significance have existed in or near the site of present-day Beijing. The first to appear in Chinese records dates back to the Western Zhou Dynasty (1027–770 BCE), when a walled village called Ji (Reeds) was built in the southwest suburbs of present-day Beijing.

In 907, the Khitans, a non-Chinese nomadic tribe, founded the Liao Dynasty and set up their capital in Yanjing, today a poetic name for Beijing that's still used for things such as the popular Yanjing Beer. From this base, the Khitans began to make inroads into the heartland of China, which had been brought under the control of the Song Dynasty in 960. The name 'Cathay' for China is said to have derived from the word 'Khitay', which is another name for the Khitan.

In 1120, the Jurchen, a Manchu tribe, formed an alliance with the Song Dynasty and five years later, defeated the Liao. The Jurchen set up their Jin (Gold) Dynasty to the southwest of present-day Beijing, turning the ruins of Yanjing into a bigger walled city, which they called 'Zhongdu' ('Middle Capital'). To the dismay of the Song rulers, the Jurchen then expanded quickly into central China, extending their control over a large swatch of land.

Genghis Khan's Mongol troops attacked Zhongdu in 1215, almost completely destroying the Jin capital. In 1267, his grandson Kublai Khan made this the capital of his Yuan Dynasty, calling his new city 'Khanbalik', or 'City of the Great Khan'. In Chinese, it was known as Dadu (Great Capital), but foreigners came to know it as Cambaluc, Marco Polo's spelling of the Mongolian word 'Khanbalik'. This was the city that the Venetian explorer described so intriguingly in *The Travels of Marco Polo*. Curiously, there is no mention of Marco Polo in Chinese history books, and some contemporary scholars wonder if the Venetian actually ever walked the streets of the old capital.

THIS PAGE (FROM TOP): An engraving of the legendary Mongol conqueror Genghis Khan; Kublai Khan, the founder of China's Yuan Dynasty, established his capital in Khanbalik, present-day Beijing.

OPPOSITE: An ancient tower looms over the old city of Beijing.

great capital

Dadu was a grand city, designed according to the ideals written in the Confucian classic, *The Rites of Zhou*—one of the earliest books on geomancy—which described the principles for the construction of homes and villages. Unfortunately, about 100 years after establishing their dynasty, the once nomadic Mongolians, softened by city life, suffered a disastrous defeat by rebels from the south, led by an itinerant Chinese monk. The Yuan Dynasty came tumbling down and its capital was torched, although the city's basic layout—evenly spaced rectilinear streets centred on a north-south axis—survived.

The new Ming Dynasty moved its capital south to Nanjing, and Dadu became known as Beiping (Northern Peace). In 1402, Zhu Di, a son of the founding emperor, usurped the throne from his young nephew. Assuming the reign title Yongle, he rebuilt a new capital on the ruins of Khanbalik, which he renamed 'Beijing' ('Northern Capital'). To inspire awe among his subjects, he began constructing the Forbidden City, a project that required some 15 years and the services of 200,000 corvée labourers.

rebellion

As with previous dynasties, the Ming Dynasty—the victim of apathetic and inefficient rulers, corrupt eunuchs, and natural disasters that fuelled rising public dissatisfaction and farmer rebellions—eventually entered a state of gradual decline. In April 1644, a peasant rebel leader named Li Zicheng managed to take over the capital, facing little resistance. Abandoned by his aides and officials, and with the rebels at the city gates, the last Ming emperor, Emperor Chongzhen, slit the throats of his concubines and retreated behind the palace, where he hung himself on a tree at the foot of Coal Hill (also known as Jingshan, or Prospect Hill), his imperial robes stained by the blood of his concubines. The tree is long gone, but the spot is still marked by a sign. His death brought the last Han Chinese-ruled dynasty to a tragic end.

While Li Zicheng's army was knocking at the gates of the imperial city, Manchu banner men—from the same Jurchen tribe that had established the earlier Jin Dynasty— were gathering strength in the north, preparing to take advantage of the chaos all around. Ironically, despite the Ming Dynasty having fortified the Great Wall, invading

Manchus easily slipped through an opening at Shanhaiguan, the eastern terminus of the wall, with the help of Wu Sangui, a disgruntled Ming general who could not bring himself to cooperate with the peasant rebel leader. According to a popular story, an angry Wu defected to the Manchu side after his mistress had been kidnapped by Li.

manchurian ascendancy

The Jurchen troops pushed Li's army out of the capital, establishing the Qing Dynasty (1644–1911). Other than insisting that the Chinese adopt the Manchu queue as a symbol of allegiance to the new dynasty, the rulers did not attempt to enforce their way of life upon the Chinese. They made an effort to retain their unique Manchu traits, with the Manchus and Chinese living in separate worlds: the Manchus in the northern, rectangular-walled half, and the Han in the southern section. Anxious to project a feeling of continuity, the Qing Dynasty did not destroy the capital, but instead, built on the Ming legacy. It carried out a far-reaching expansion of the Forbidden City, building wonderful mansions, and magnificent garden retreats in the western suburbs.

Qianlong ascended the throne in 1736 and remained in control for six decades, a period considered by many to be the city's golden era. The emperor beefed up the military while at the same time promoting literature and the arts. Qianlong was also interested in Tibetan Buddhism, and supported the construction of lamaseries in the capital. While he forbade the Chinese from converting to Roman Catholicism (Jesuit Matteo Ricci was the first Catholic priest to arrive in the capital in 1603), he welcomed the skills of foreign priests in the service of the court. Qianlong also left his mark on the city by building new sites, many of which exist to this day.

It's said that the emperor would sometimes sneak out of the palace, making incognito visits to restaurants, temples and shops just outside the gates of the Forbidden City. According to one popular story, it was Chinese New Year's eve in 1752, and all the shops in Qianmen's normally bustling Dazhalan area were closed as shopowners were busy settling their annual accounts. However, the lanterns at one small wine shop attracted three well-dressed patrons. Wang Ruifu, the owner, politely ushered them upstairs and personally served them his best dishes and wine. When one of the guests

asked the name of the shop, Wang answered, 'I don't have a name.' One of the men gratefully said to the owner, 'At this hour, you are probably the only shop still open. Why not call it "Du Yi Chu" ("The Only Place")?'

Wang soon forgot about the incident, and so, was surprised days later when eunuchs from the imperial city showed up to present him with a wooden plaque emblazoned with three characters: 'Du Yi Chu'. It was only then that the shop owner realised that one of the three guests dining at his store that evening was none other than Emperor Qianlong. Wang fell on his knees, kowtowing to show his gratitude. Today, the sign bearing Qianlong's calligraphy sits in a glass case in the restaurant, testament to the fact that Du Yi Chu is one of the oldest eateries in the capital, and dates back some two and a half centuries.

foreigners at the gates

The imperial court proved unwilling to modernise and was unable to match the military prowess of the foreign powers of the day, resulting in a series of humiliating defeats, each of which brought new demands for concessions and unequal treaties. Toward the end of the 19th century, the government had no choice but to cave in to foreign demands for a permanent presence in the capital, and soon the foreign Legation Quarter sprang up just southeast of the Forbidden City, bringing in to the capital a new style of Western architecture and irrevocable changes.

In the mid-1890s, the Harmonious Fists, a secret martial society known in English as the Boxers, began to emerge, adopting a strongly anti-foreign attitude. The Boxers, who claimed magical powers that enabled them to withstand blows by swords and bullets, began to attack foreign missionaries and Chinese converts to Christianity. In 1900, with a quiet wink from the notorious Empress Dowager Cixi, duped into thinking the Boxers could resolve her foreign 'problem', the group laid siege to the Legation Quarter, home to much of the foreign community in Beijing. The incident was poorly portrayed in a movie titled *55 Days at Peking*, which starred Charlton Heston.

THIS PAGE (FROM TOP): A late 19th-century photo of a group of Manchu gunners resting; Empress Dowager Cixi, an avid fan of early photography, poses for the camera in 1903.

OPPOSITE: A view of the Forbidden City, dating back to the late 19th and early 20th century.

The siege ended after a multinational force, made up of troops from eight allied nations, marched into Beijing, sending the Boxers scattering and the Imperial Court fleeing in disguise to the safety of Xi'an, in Shaanxi province. The Qing offered to pay a Boxer Indemnity, and the emperor and the empress dowager quietly returned to the capital. The foreign troops remained in Beijing and surrounding areas for a year, harassing Chinese citizens and looting cultural artefacts. The ancient capital would never be the same again.

Although the Qing had reached an accommodation with the foreign forces in China, its problems did not end. Its failure to deal with foreign encroachment fuelled growing public resentment against the Manchu court, already reeling from an array of internal problems. Peasant rebellions rose around the country—a clear sign that the Mandate of Heaven was about to fall from the hands of the Qing emperor. In October 1911, a revolution brought the imperial system to an end.

warlords and republicans

On February 12, 1912, the regent Prince Chun, on behalf of his son, the boy emperor Pu Yi, issued an official decree acknowledging that imperial rule had come to an end. Under an agreement with the new Republican government—helmed by its first president Yuan Shikai, a former powerful general in the Manchu army—the court was still permitted to remain within the Forbidden City, the Summer Palace, and the Imperial Resort in neighbouring Chengde.

In 1915, Yuan attempted to revive the imperial system, with himself as the new Son of Heaven, and even ordered new custom-

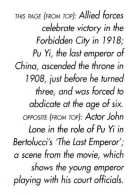

THIS PAGE (FROM TOP): Allied forces celebrate victory in the Forbidden City in 1918; Pu Yi, the last emperor of China, ascended the throne in 1908, just before he turned three, and was forced to abdicate at the age of six. OPPOSITE (FROM TOP): Actor John Lone in the role of Pu Yi in Bertolucci's 'The Last Emperor'; a scene from the movie, which shows the young emperor playing with his court officials.

made imperial robes and chinaware to mark his new reign. Yuan's plan met with fierce opposition, and the former general died the following year, his dream unfulfilled.

Pu Yi made a brief comeback in 1917 when Zhang Xun (an imperial loyalist known as the Pigtail General because he made his soldiers retain their Manchu queues) attempted to restore the monarchy. The farcical attempt failed within just a few days after another warlord counter-attacked, hand-dropping bombs from an airplane into the Forbidden City. In 1924, Feng Yuxiang, a warlord better known internationally as the Christian General (he made his soldiers read the Bible and baptised them with a garden hose) forced the emperor to vacate the Forbidden City. Pu Yi's story is told in Bernardo Bertolucci's classic film, *The Last Emperor*, starring John Lone and Joan Chen.

A victim of a succession of rulers, the grand old capital did not fare well during the next few decades. However, it was a period of excitement. Students marched to Tiananmen Square in May 1919 to protest the Versailles Conference, which ceded Germany's territories in China to the Japanese. Leading intellectuals, scholars and artists flocked to the city, debating China's state of affairs. The most outspoken shouted out, 'Down with the Confucian shop!' and called for Mr Science and Mr Democracy to take the seat of the great sage. There was a movement away from the highly stylised, classical tradition to a vernacular, accessible form of written Chinese. It was also around this time that a little-known Hunanese farm boy named Mao Zedong worked as an assistant librarian at Peking University, where he met lecturers Li Dazhao and Chen Duxiu, both of whom would go on to be founding members of the Chinese Communist Party (CCP).

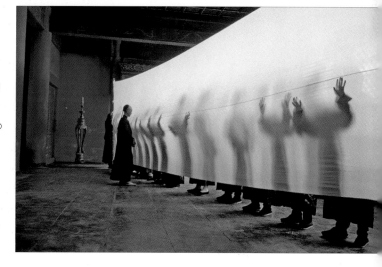

In 1921, a group of intellectuals, influenced by the Russian Revolution, met in Shanghai to establish the CCP. From these small beginnings, a Communist movement gradually began to take hold throughout the country (Mao was the secretary-general for the CCP branch in Hunan). In 1923, the CCP allied with Sun Yat Sen's

...Beijing became the capital of New China on October 1, 1949...

Kuomintang (KMT), or Nationalist Party, in order to form a united front against the warlords in northern China. However, after Sun's death in 1925, its new leader, Generalissimo Chiang Kai Shek, soon launched a purge of Communists within the KMT.

The KMT government moved the capital back to Nanjing in 1928, and Beijing was again renamed Beiping. During this period, the city's heritage suffered greatly due to neglect and vandalism. Meanwhile, Chiang decided to put an end to the Communist challenge once and for all, launching a blockade against the Communist stronghold in the mountains of Jiangxi province, known as the Jiangxi Soviet. The blockade forced the Communists to flee the area, setting the army of some 100,000 on the now famous Long March to its new headquarters in Yan'an, in China's northwest. By the time they arrived there in 1936, only about a tenth of the original troops remained, but it was from this revolutionary base that Mao's leadership within the party was reaffirmed, and the Communist movement was to re-emerge as a powerful challenge to the Nationalists.

In 1937, Japan used the pretence of a Chinese attack against Japanese troops to justify opening fire on Nationalist troops on the Marco Polo Bridge in southwest Beijing. The event, known as the Marco Polo Bridge Incident, was the beginning of a brutal eight-year occupation of the city. The KMT was forced to move its government inland to Chongqing in Sichuan province, and to form a temporary alliance with the Red Army to fight the Japanese. The Japanese surrender in 1945 was followed by four years of bitter civil war between the declining KMT forces and the resurgent Red Army.

the red revolution

On January 31, 1949, the Red Army marched victoriously into Beiping; the KMT, on the other hand, fled across the Formosa Straits to the island of Taiwan. Beijing became the capital of New China on October 1, 1949 when Mao Zedong, by then chairman of the CCP, stood on the rostrum of the Gate of Heavenly Peace and declared to millions of cheering Chinese, 'The Chinese people have stood up!'

THIS PAGE: A night scene at the Gate of Heavenly Peace, the entrance to the Forbidden City.
OPPOSITE: The Museum of the War of Chinese People's Resistance Against Japanese Aggression.

For several decades, China's capital continued to be known to the outside world as 'Peking' or 'Pei-ching' before the pinyin spelling of 'Beijing' was adopted. Meanwhile, the city underwent wrenching changes. Ancient structures made way for bland, box-like Soviet-style architecture and urban factories. The city walls were torn down—except for the odd gate or tower—to make way for a new ring road, a subway and a massive underground bomb shelter. During the Cultural Revolution (1966–76), Red Guards damaged temples and historical sites, anxious to destroy 'the four olds': old customs, old habits, old culture and old thinking. Residents of the city's magnificent old courtyard homes were pushed aside to make room for worker families. It was during this time that many of these structures, originally intended to house one family, were damaged when they were subdivided to accommodate several families.

red capitalism

Chairman Mao passed away in September 1976 at the age of 82, and just three years later, Deng Xiaoping, who had emerged as the new strongman of China, began implementing his 'black cat, white cat' theory, which argued that it did not matter whether a cat was black or white; what was important was that it caught mice. In other words, whatever works in improving the economy and the lives of the people is good, no matter what you call it. China's rulers launched reform and opening up, and 'To get rich is glorious!' became the nation's new battle cry.

In the late 1980s, Chinese intellectuals took advantage of the country's opening up to passionately engage in an open and lively debate about issues of national interest that were obstructing the country's development. In the summer of 1989, hundreds of thousands of Chinese students—hailing from cities and provinces all over the country—began expressing their frustration with the plethora of problems facing the nation at that time. Foreign investment slowed temporarily, but trade was soon back on track and the economy began chalking up impressive double digit growth as China became the factory of the world and exports hit record levels.

'To get rich is glorious!'

...one of the most ambitious urban makeovers the world has ever seen.

By the late 1990s, Chinese society was undergoing amazing changes. Hawkers of the world's top-end designer items flocked to the city's impressive new malls. The Chinese themselves engaged in a collective makeover, trading in their Mao jackets for branded goods from Gucci and Prada. And while smearing on a little lipstick would have landed a stern rebuke during the 1960s and 1970s, Yves Saint Laurent, Chanel and Christian Dior took over the ground floors of the city's new department stores, with Beijing's savvy new generation plunking down the equivalent of an office worker's monthly salary just for an imported lipstick or blusher.

olympic glory

Beijing won the right to host the 2008 Olympics, setting the city off on one of the most ambitious urban makeovers the world has ever seen. This ongoing transformation— estimated to cost more than RMB150 billion (US$20 billion)—extends from fast rising urban business districts to the renewal of lowly hutong (or Beijing's quaint alleyways), remaking the layout of a city that has not changed much since imperial times.

Activity is everywhere. Glassy skyscrapers and posh modern apartment buildings are rising seemingly overnight, carpets of grass are being laid around the city, new ring roads and subway lines have been constructed and extended, and sidewalks have been paved with shiny new tiles. Leading names in international architecture are tripping over one another to snap up some of the immense projects planned for Beijing, a trend that is expected to drastically remake the face of the old capital.

Unfortunately, huge swatches of old hutong and hallmark courtyard houses have also been razed to make way for new housing, business complexes, hotels, and Olympic venues. There are signs that the city government is now making efforts to retain some of Beijing's proud history, by declaring some hutong protected sites, remodelling or rebuilding courtyard houses in a few areas, and collecting the original city wall bricks to rebuild a small section of the old city wall. A number of citizens have also banded together, forming NGOs dedicated to the preservation of the city's past.

THIS PAGE: *A model poses with traditional red lanterns at a contest for up-and-coming fashion designers.*

OPPOSITE: *Visitors look across a model of Beijing at the Urban Planning Museum. The imposing National Stadium, known as the 'Bird's Nest', is on the right.*

back to the future

Today, the city remains a hodgepodge of cultures, tottering on the wall of past and present, as if uncertain in which direction to move.

Every morning, Beijing's numerous parks are crowded with people doing their exercises: taiqi, martial arts, badminton, and even ballroom and disco dancing. Elderly Beijing men pass the time by playing with their kites or crickets, or admiring their birds hanging in ornate cages from tree branches. Some are absorbed in a game of Chinese chess, surrounded by a dozen friends and onlookers craning their necks to catch a glimpse of what's happening on the board.

The streets are packed with a steady stream of cars—from the locally made Geely to foreign brands such as Audi, Mercedes-Benz, and even the occasional Mini Cooper or Hummer—all competing for space with bicycles, still the preferred means of transport for many Beijing residents (although flashy mountain bikes have taken the place of the once coveted 'Flying Pigeons').

THIS PAGE (FROM TOP): Once forbidden by the Communist Party, the game of mahjong has returned with a vengeance; a girl waits for a public bus on one of Beijing's busy streets.

OPPOSITE: A door opens, revealing the rich red walls of the Forbidden City.

Walk around just about any part of the city and you will find a bevy of shops, from small mom-and-pop ventures selling old Beijing snacks and daily necessities to glitzy malls showcasing the best designer products the world has to offer. Take your pick of old and new, from cotton-padded shoes and roasted sweet potatoes to Tiffany's jewellery, Prada bags, Bentley automobiles, and the latest boarding gear from Quiksilver. At meal times, local Chinese and foreign expatriates rub elbows at the city's countless eateries, ranging from little holes in the wall selling exotic southern foods to chic fusion restaurants in new high rises or complexes.

Possibly because they cannot resurrect the old city walls and hutong, Beijingers are showing a renewed

...tottering on the wall of past and present, as if uncertain in which direction to move.

interest in the capital's colourful past. Photographers and artists race around the city, anxious to record Beijing's old hutong, courtyard houses and old way of life before these completely disappear. Laozihao, or famous old brand name shops and restaurants, are sprucing up their image and attracting a growing number of customers nostalgic for the good old days. The city has also seen an increase in the number of restaurants offering old Beijing specialties, dishes that were until recently on the verge of extinction. The once-deserted theatres, which in the past used to stage performances of traditional Beijing storytelling and comedy dialogues, are again packed with laughing audiences. And classic plays about old Beijing, such as Lao She's *Teahouse* or Cao Yu's *Peking Man*, are now playing to young, enthusiastic audiences.

In a wonderful essay on the changes that have taken place in Beijing, titled 'City Without Walls', Beijing author and culture critic Zha Jianying tells of a friend who is well known for his graceful, nostalgic stories about the city. 'Modern Beijing,' she quotes him as saying, 'is a city where it's impossible to find a spot to hang up one's birdcage.'

To understand what he means, says Zha, you have to know about an older, more classic Beijing image: 'A gentleman with his tamed birds in a bamboo cage hanging on a branch in a quiet park or in a merry teahouse, or simply in his own courtyard. It is the quintessential image of leisure and a certain type of cultivation. The birdcage is a symbol whose disappearance would mean that a certain lifestyle and a whole set of values had gone with it.'

As Beijing marches into the future and takes its rightful place as a global metropolis of the 21st century, there is increasing hope that the city will find a reasonable balance between past and present, and that there will always be a tree on which to hang that birdcage.

THIS PAGE: *A window in a Burberry's shop offers a reflection of a new building going up in the city, which has seen a rising middle class with enough cash to buy designer goods and luxury apartments.*

OPPOSITE: *A gallery visitor poses in front of a piece of art at the Beijing 798 Art Zone.*

cultural capital

Beijing is the cultural capital of China, with every type of artist drawn to the city, a trend that can be traced back to dynastic days. But, for decades, few were able to get ahead in a country emphasising Chinese Social Realism. Art took a backseat to politics in 1942, when Mao Zedong proclaimed that 'art must serve politics'. From that time on, art was not something reserved for the upper classes, but a tool of and for the masses. For the next three decades, art was put on hold.

And, while art returned with a vengeance after China kicked off its reform and opening period in 1979, it's still by no means free. Politics no longer rules art, but it still manages to interfere, with artists often forced to deal with censors. However, as international consumer tastes—and not Maoist dogma—increasingly dictate artistic trends, Chinese artists have to a certain extent been freed to make a great artistic leap forward that has resulted in unprecedented new art forms.

...combines music, dance, martial arts, acrobatics and acting.

singing for survival

Beijing opera, better known to the outside world as Peking opera, is a rich cultural tradition, an offshoot of China's myriad opera styles that date back more than 1,000 years. Known in Chinese as jingxi (theatre of the capital), this quintessential Chinese art form combines music, dance, martial arts, acrobatics and acting. It's also on the list of endangered Chinese art forms.

What we call Peking opera today is a relatively young art form dating back to 1790, when opera troupes from Anhui province performed in the capital as part of Emperor Qianlong's 80th birthday celebrations. Local audiences couldn't get enough, and new troupes began to form, with budding actors recruited from poor families who sold their sons to opera schools affiliated with Beijing's main companies. Training was harsh, and beatings an unquestioned part of the curriculum. This sad tradition is vividly portrayed in Chen Kaige's film classic *Farewell My Concubine*.

To many, Cheng Changgeng (1811–80), an excellent laosheng, or 'old male' actor, is considered the father of Beijing opera. He integrated different components of regional theatre into Beijing opera, brought the art form to a new artistic level, and improved the image of performers. As opera gained popularity with the masses, theatres sprung up in the Qianmen area of Beijing. Several opera schools led by famous actors began to flourish, and a number of acting families also rose to prominence.

Officials, however, looked down on Beijing opera. The Manchu leaders had set up a court training school for actors in the 18th century, but it trained students only for the more aristocratic Kunqu operas. Furthermore, only eunuchs or famous actors from southern China were allowed to perform for the royal family. An exception was made in 1860, when, in celebration of Emperor Xianfeng's birthday, the imperial court invited performers from the capital to stage Beijing opera performances in the Forbidden City. However, these were cut short when invading British and French soldiers occupied

THIS PAGE: *The interior of a traditional Beijing opera house. The ancient art, known in Chinese as the theatre of the capital, is on the verge of extinction, a victim of the more popular modern cultures.*

OPPOSITE: *Opera performers go through their acrobatic moves in what is called China's quintessential art form.*

Beijing, forcing the court to flee to the imperial family's summer retreat in nearby Chengde. By the time the threat ended, Xianfeng had died and conservative forces were again holding sway in the imperial court. Beijing opera was once again banned. In 1884, Empress Dowager Cixi, an avid opera fan, constructed two large stages in the Summer Palace and a small stage in her own living quarters. History intervened yet again, when soldiers from eight foreign powers entered the capital to put down the Boxer Uprising in 1900, razing Beijing's grand theatres.

Opera survived nevertheless; pre-eminent among the performers then was female impersonator Mei Lanfang, whose fame stretched as far as Europe and the United States. Mei boosted the status of actors and, more importantly, broke the gender line in the theatre by bravely accepting actress Xue Yanqin as his student in the 1930s. Prior to this, there were few mixed gender troupes in Beijing opera, with female roles normally played by men. Xue went on to become one of the greatest performers in Beijing opera.

Opera fared well in the early years of Communist rule when actors enjoyed a newfound respectability. Determined that men would play male roles and women female ones, officials banned the old opera schools and set up new schools admitting both boys and girls. They also banned the use of caiqiao, stilted shoes that enabled actors to mimic the gait of women with bound feet, and changed the content of some operas, in line with the Communist dictum that all art should serve politics.

Unfortunately, Beijing opera was not able to withstand the political upheavals that began in the 1950s. The first blow came during the Hundred Flowers Movement in 1957, when the party attacked the 'feudal' aspects of the art, whose plots were based on traditional stories and myths. Attempts were made to introduce modern themes, settings and costumes, changes that were not welcome by audiences. During the Cultural Revolution, Red Guards burnt opera scripts, recordings and books about opera. Traditional opera stars—with the exception of a few revolutionary actors—were hunted

THIS PAGE (FROM TOP): *Children absorbed in an opera performance. According to a popular saying, 'each word is a song, each movement a dance'; a performer peers into a mirror as he puts the finishing touches on his colourful make-up.*
OPPOSITE: *A sumptuous scene from a popular Beijing opera.*

down and humiliated. Dubbing traditional opera 'ghost plays', Jiang Qing, wife of
Chairman Mao Zedong, replaced them with eight model revolutionary operas. Only
scripts approved by the former actress were allowed to be staged; these had to reflect
class struggle, promote proletarian interests and denounce bourgeois villains. (Ironically,
these 'revolutionary' operas enjoyed a popular revival in the 1990s among
theatregoers, apparently nostalgic for the 'good old days'.)

Opera enjoyed a brief resurgence when China opened up in the late 1970s,
thanks to Chinese leader Deng Xiaoping's love of the traditional art form. But this revival

would prove to be short-lived. In the 1980s, opera was soon being submerged by new forms of entertainment that appealed to a generation of younger Chinese not weaned on this intricate style of art.

Each year, graduates of the various schools desert the opera to become nightclub singers—a profession with low social status, but which pays much more. With low salaries paid for a tough regimen that begins as early as the age of eight, it's no wonder the dropout rate is so high. The average actor makes RMB1,000–2,000 (US$132–264) a month, as much as a worker in a state-owned factory. Some underpaid performers moonlight in restaurants where their well-trained voices compete with the chitchat of diners and the clashing of chopsticks against rice bowls. Others don colourful costumes to pose for photographs with tourists at famous Beijing sites, while some troupes have been reduced to performing at funerals.

Still, the fat lady has not quite finished singing; the ancient art form is struggling to reinvent itself to compete with new forms of entertainment. Plays that once lasted up to six hours are cut to a more palatable two hours, props are added to the normally sparse stage, and acting techniques are incorporated from modern theatre, cinema and even television soaps. Purists, however, lament that such reforms are made not for the art, but for the box office, and could alienate serious opera fans instead of attracting a new following.

And while some see Western tourism as the saviour of Beijing opera, others argue that actors who perform largely for tourists give less than stellar performances, since audiences can't tell the difference anyway. For instance, the Li Yuan Theatre is crowded with foreign tour groups every night, but the show seldom departs from the diet of short excerpts full of impressive acrobatics, more often than not action-packed Monkey King stories easily digested by audiences who do not understand Chinese.

It's difficult for people to understand the obsession ximi (opera fans) have for the art. To fans, music is the heart of Chinese opera; the term 'tingxi', which means 'going to the opera', literally means 'listening to an opera'. Genuine ximi will pay to watch the same operas over and over again, singing along inwardly, eyes closed, yet knowing exactly when to open their eyes to watch a particularly stirring gesture. A story is told of a businessman of the 1930s who went bankrupt buying expensive tickets to watch Mei Lanfang play the role of the beautiful Yang Guifei. Ironically, with foreign tourism driving up the average price of an opera ticket to around RMB53 (US$7)—triple what it was a few years ago and several days' income for some locals—many loyal ximi cannot afford even a back row seat.

contemporary art

It was not too long ago that any mention of Chinese art would conjure visions of blue Ming vases, Qing Dynasty scroll paintings, or ancient bronzes. The images have long since changed. Chinese art today is made up of Plexiglas sculptures of Beijing's working class; innovative installation art; pop, satiric portraits of Chairman Mao; often outrageous performance art; and cynical paintings depicting modern society. The country's emergence as an up-and-coming superpower is now turning the world's attention to Chinese contemporary art, and its artists are winning accolades for their realistic portrayal of life in modern China.

Indeed, China's contemporary artists are now among the hottest in the world, thanks to a growing global interest and a gradually rising appreciation by a rapidly expanding middle class at home. As buyers scurry to grab some of the best works for

THIS PAGE: *At the Beijing 798 Art Zone, a woman studies paintings by Chinese artist Zou Cao portraying caricatures of US president George W. Bush and Osama bin Laden.*

OPPOSITE: *Stilt walkers pose for photos outside the Dongyue Temple during a Chinese New Year fair. At other attractions, visitors may chance upon opera artistes in colourful costumes, posing with tourists.*

their collections, prices being paid for works by top Chinese artists—barely known five years ago—have doubled, tripled and quadrupled in recent years, leading one gallery owner to liken the hunger for new Chinese art to a gold rush.

New Chinese artists are proving that great upheavals can sometimes result in great art. And with the country's recent turbulent history, Chinese artists have found a fertile ground for their creativity that is paying off handsomely. In September 2006, for example, Chen Danqing's 'Street Theater', a 1991 work with a theme related to the 1989 democracy protests, fetched nearly RMB11 million (US$1.5 million). 'Tiananmen Square' (1993), Zhang Xiaogang's similarly themed work, pulled in RMB17 million (US$2.3 million), which auction house Christie's said was the highest ever paid in the international auction market for an oil painting by a living Chinese artist. But not for long. Shortly after, another painting by a Chinese artist sold for more than RMB20 million (US$2.7 million).

THIS PAGE (FROM TOP): Artist Zhang Xiaogang with his painting; a performance artist in front of photographs at a Beijing 798 Art Festival.

OPPOSITE: Sculptures by artist Ren Hongwei titled '1.3 Billion' on display at the festival.

Art critics say the trend could not have been realised had the government not softened its attitude regarding artists, many of whom faced censorship and persecution throughout the 1990s. This more tolerant attitude—with some exceptions—has made it possible for many Chinese artists to emerge from a sort of 'underground' existence to the international mainstream, winning critical acclaim for the arts in China.

Some critics fear that success may have come too fast and too easily, with the buyers of this new genre often unfamiliar with what they're buying—or even the names of the artists. Other critics complain that today's art is created primarily for export, and that form is more important than quality.

Still, contemporary Chinese art is no flash in the pan. With China's rise as a world power and the growing wealth and recognition of artists, local artists are not just producing good art; they are also becoming more self-confident and independent enough to set future trends in the booming art market.

New Chinese artists are proving that great upheavals can sometimes result in great art.

music

Beijing is home to an interesting live music scene, from rock to jazz to hip hop, that is exploding with the fast expanding number of clubs and bars and the growing sophistication of local music fans. China's indigenous music got off the ground with musician-singer Cui Jian, who became internationally famous in the late 1980s with his hit song, the somewhat rebellious *Nothing to My Name*. A trained classical musician who started his career as a trumpeter with the Beijing Philharmonic, Cui became obsessed with Western rock and roll in the 1980s after listening to tapes brought into China by foreign tourists and friends. For years, Cui was not allowed to perform at concerts and was even prevented from playing in small jazz clubs around Beijing. The restrictions on Cui, known as the father of Chinese rock, were recently lifted, but some rock concerts—New York rapper Jay-Z's debut Shanghai performance, for instance—are still banned.

Rock and roll has been rumbling around Beijing for 20 years now, and about 400 active rock bands perform regularly in bars and clubs around the city. Still, musicians find it tough to survive. Kaiser Kuo, one of the founders of heavy-metal group Tang Dynasty, writes that Chinese—even relatively hip urbanites—do not generally like rock, and lean towards slick, sticky pop music from Hong Kong and Taiwan. While rock has developed a 'devoted core following', it's still a 'peripheral phenomenon' even in Beijing.

There are signs that this may be changing. In recent years, more international musicians—including The Rolling Stones, Eric Clapton, The Roots, Sonic Youth, and Ziggy Marley—have performed in China. Beijing's weeklong outdoor Midi Music Festival, held in Haidian each May, attracts tens of thousands of fans. Among the 90 bands appearing in 2007 were Brain Failure, Catcher in the Rye, New Pants, Yaksa and Mian Kong. Foreign participants included England's Imogen Heap, and David Stewart (of Eurythmics fame) and Rock Fabulous from the United States.

THIS PAGE: The annual Midi Music Festival, which features local and international bands.

OPPOSITE: A man walks past a photograph of Chinese movie star Gong Li at Beijing's National Film Museum.

cinema

For more than three decades after the Chinese Communists came to power in 1949, Chinese filmmakers turned out primarily propaganda films that had little, if any, artistic value. This all changed in the 1980s, when the Fifth Generation of Chinese directors, such as Zhang Yimou, Chen Kaige and Tian Zhuangzhuang, began turning out poignant films with China's recent past and rapidly-changing present as backdrops.

Zhang Yimou's directorial debut in 1987, *Red Sorghum*, introduced the beautiful Gong Li to movie audiences around the world. The former factory worker went on to direct other classics such as *Raise the Red Lantern*, *Ju Dou*, *To Live*, and *Hero*, an ambitious cinematic effort that was nominated for an Oscar in 2003. In 1993, Chen Kaige made *Farewell My Concubine*, the tale of love between two opera stars that spans pre-liberation China up to the heady days of the 1970s.

It would not take long before international film festivals were highlighting mainland Chinese efforts by Zhang and Chen, and younger directors such as Zhang Yuan, Jia Zhangke and Wang Xiaoshuai. More often than not, these films were not initially approved for screening at home. Recently, *Tuya's Marriage*, by Chinese director Wang Quanan, turned out to be a surprise winner of the 2007 Golden Bear for Best Film at the 57th Berlin International Film Festival. Wang's film drew critical acclaim for depicting the heroic effort of a herder in Inner Mongolia to keep her family together against all odds.

The most recent trend, however, has been toward the production of the blockbuster, a movement that has resulted in uneven results. With the chance to pull in domestic receipts, local film producers have been willing to boost investments in larger projects, such as Chen's *The Promise* and Zhang's megahits *Hero* and *Curse of the Golden Flower*, the latter a lavish effort about a despicable royal family during the Tang Dynasty, starring Gong Li and Hong Kong movie idol Chow Yun Fat.

Despite the excellence of contemporary cinema in China, the industry continues to be hamstrung by government censors, restrictions, protectionism and bureaucracy. Scripts have to be vetted by censors before shooting begins, and many topics remain taboo. The government limits foreign imports to 20 a year, and some of the best never make it to local screens because they're deemed objectionable.

Summer Palace, a love story with the 1989 student protests as a backdrop, and containing explicit sex scenes, was banned after it was submitted to the Palme d'Or at the Cannes Film Festival without first getting a government nod, and director Lou Ye has been banned from making any new films in China for five years. The censors, however, have not succeeded in preventing local movie fans from watching what they want. *Summer Palace* was easily available on the shelves of counterfeit DVD shops, and Hollywood's *Brokeback Mountain*, rejected for its homosexual nature, was hawked on the streets by enterprising DVD sellers just as the film was screened in the United States.

THIS PAGE (FROM TOP): *A smiling Zhang Ziyi listens to director Zhang Yimou at a press conference to promote his blockbuster, 'Hero'; Chen Kaige's 'Farewell My Concubine', starring the late Hong Kong star, Leslie Cheung.*
OPPOSITE: *The National Ballet of China rehearses the ballet 'Raise the Red Lantern' at the Théâtre du Châtelet in Paris.*

dance

Unlike other arts that were officially rehabilitated soon after the end of the Cultural Revolution, modern dance, like rock music, remained suspect and suppressed, and had to wait in the wings for another decade to return to the stage.

Ballet debuted in China just after the 1917 Russian Revolution, when emigrant ballet teachers escaped to China. In 1954, Dai Ailian, a Trinidad-born, London-raised student of ballet and modern dance, established the Beijing Dance School, which in 1959 evolved into the Central Ballet of China and later the National Ballet of China.

The National Ballet of China puts on regular performances of famous Western ballets, including *The Nutcracker*, *Swan Lake* and *Giselle*, but it is perhaps best at fusing Western and Chinese forms. *Raise the Red Lantern*, based on Zhang Yimou's movie, is one of many examples where ballet and traditional Chinese opera converge. Another is the very popular *The Red Detachment of Women*, a Maoist propaganda work from 1964 about a farm girl who joins the workers' revolution. In recent years especially, there has been a nostalgia for Cultural Revolution favourites, such as *The Red Detachment of Women* and *The White-Haired Girl*.

The explosion of rock music in China has resulted in a growing interest in jiewu (street dancing). One new college, the Beijing Contemporary Music Institute, even offers a college degree in this genre. In a large dance studio, teenagers in baggy pants stare intently into the wall-

length mirror, their bodies moving, snake-like. They are taught hip hop, break dancing, locking, popping, punk and cruising by teachers from South Korea—apparently the best street dancers in the region. Baseball caps jauntily placed on their heads, the students move from popping and then to house, their legs resembling spaghetti, never completely leaving the floor, looking as if they're stuck there by bubble gum.

a taste of tradition

Beijing may be the modern spelling for the Chinese capital, but mention roast duck, and most people still think 'Peking Duck', a local specialty prepared by revolving a young duckling on a spit in an oven. Peking roast duck dates back to the Yuan Dynasty (1206–1368), when it was first listed among the imperial dishes in *The Complete Recipes for Dishes and Beverages*, written in 1330 by Hu Sihui, an inspector of the imperial kitchen. It continued to be a popular dish when the capital of the succeeding Ming Dynasty was reestablished in Beijing in the early 15th century, and in the Qianlong period (1736–96), it would prove to be a favourite among the upper classes, with scholars inspired to write poems and other words of praise after enjoying a particularly delicious meal of roast duck.

According to local historical records, Beijing's earliest duck restaurant was Bianyifang, established during Ming Emperor Jiajing's reign (1522–66). A second restaurant, Quanjude, opened its doors in 1864, during the reign of the Qing emperor Tongzhi. Both restaurants are now state-owned, and are still roasting up ducks at various locations around Beijing. However, they've been overtaken by a bevy of smaller, arguably more professional restaurants, such as Yawang (Duck King), Dadong, Likang, and Li Qun.

Duck aficionados swear that the best birds come from farms located near the Summer Palace, which locals say is blessed with rich earth and excellent water. The Qinglongqiao Duck Farm has been raising ducks along the Jingma Irrigation Canal,

THIS PAGE (FROM TOP): A Chinese dancer performs at the closing ceremony of Beijing's China Fashion Week, one of the city's trendiest annual events; roast Peking Duck, the dish that made Beijing famous.

OPPOSITE (FROM TOP): A small shop displays piles of pan-fried bread, a popular Beijing staple; Beijing's night food market.

which runs out of Kunming Lake in the Summer Palace, for about 50 years. Farmers point out that the water that is used to feed the ducks comes from nearby Yuquan Mountain—the same water that the emperors used to drink.

Many of Beijing's other popular and delightful foods also date back to imperial days. But unlike roast duck, these local delicacies are prepared by itinerant hawkers who can be found pushing their carts along the city's back streets.

Jianbing, a stuffed pancake, is one of the most ubiquitous street foods. Its egg and flour batter is spooned onto a round flat cooking surface that sits on a pushcart. A small wooden 'rake' is used to spread the batter in a circular motion, starting from the centre outwards. An egg is then cracked and the spreading procedure continues, then chopped spring onion is tossed over the paper-thin crepe and some sweet bean sauce and chilli sauce brushed on top. The crepe is then turned over several times to form a square.

A street snack that's especially good on a cold winter day is the roasted sweet potato. The hawker hangs his golden potatoes inside a re-fitted oil drum, heated by round briquettes of burning coal at the bottom. The slow roasting inside this unique oven, which has no controls, makes the sweet potatoes melt in your mouth.

Another winter favourite among children in northern China is sugar-coated fruit. Traditionally, slightly sour haws, chosen precisely for their tartness, are used, and taste wonderful coated with a hard sugar glaze. Today, all sorts of fruit—including strawberries, kiwis and bananas—are skewered and glazed.

Mahua, literally 'braided horse tail' because that's what it resembles, is a piece of crispy, deep-fried twisted dough. You'll find these golden 'braids' piled several feet high on bicycle carts throughout the streets of Beijing.

culinary revolution

Beijing has undergone a culinary revolution over the past decade, with restaurants from around China and all over the world flinging open their doors across the city. The venues—from chic restaurants to hole-in-the-wall eateries hidden in Beijing's hutong—are part of the fun.

The city has come a long way from the early 1990s, when eating out often meant dining at one of the ubiquitous Cantonese or Sichuan eateries, usually drab affairs with dim fluorescent lighting and plastic garbage bag tablecloths that stuck to your forearms.

One of the pioneers in the city's culinary renaissance is American entrepreneur and long-time Beijing resident Lawrence Brahm. In 2000, Brahm spearheaded the popularisation of what he calls 'Beijing retro chic', when he launched Red Capital Club in a restored old courtyard house. The restaurant, with its post-liberation themed bar and Qing-style dining room, was an immediate hit. Brahm claims that his chefs are veterans of the kitchens of Zhongnanhai, headquarters of former top Communist officials, and that they whip up the favourite dishes of the Communist pantheon.

Going even further back in time, Baijia Dazhaimen conjures up the grandeur of the past even before any of its Manchu imperial dishes is served. The restaurant is housed in a mansion that was once the residence of Prince Li, son of the first Qing emperor, and as guests enter, young women in colourful traditional Manchu attire speak an old imperial court greeting: 'Nin jixiang', or 'May you have good fortune.'

On the other hand, one could be forgiven for walking right past Zhang Qun Jia (Zhang Qun's Home), a small restaurant on the narrow and winding Yandai Bending Street, just off the Rear Lakes. There is no sign above the restaurant, only a fading brown door with the number '5' written on it. Artist Zhang Qun meant it to be a place to entertain her friends, but it soon turned into a one-table restaurant serving the delicately prepared, home-style specialties of her native Suzhou. The organic chicken comes from the Inner Mongolia grasslands, and the evergreen vegetables are shipped by train from

THIS PAGE (FROM TOP): Upmarket eatery, GREEN T. HOUSE; the restaurant features a minimalist design that revolves around a white theme.

OPPOSITE: An elegant table setting at Beijing's GREEN T. HOUSE.

her hometown. This traditional house, with natural light shining through the small skylight, has the cosy feeling of a friend's home.

Beijing's laozihao, or old brand name shops, did not escape the demolition crews that tore down the old Qianmen district in 2006 to make way for the high rises and shopping malls that are being slapped up. But a dozen well-known restaurants, some dating back more than a century, have found refuge in a large traditional courtyard house near the Rear Lakes, where the old Menkuang Hutong of Qianmen has been 'recreated' as 'Jiumen Xiaochi', or 'Nine Gates Snacks' (referring to the nine gates that once graced the old city wall). Stalls have been set up on both sides of the indoor 'hutong', with diners sitting at traditional wooden tables and chairs. Around them, black-and-white photos of old Beijing adorn the walls. The eateries here include Baodu Feng, an old Beijing Muslim family restaurant specialising in flash-boiled tripe since the Qing Dynasty; Niangao Qian, known for its sticky rice layered with red bean paste as well as ludagun ('donkey rolling on the ground'), the most popular sticky rice snack made by the Hui, or Chinese Muslims; Yangtou Ma, renowned for its thin sliced meat from boiled lamb's head; Doufunao Bai, which serves up a soft bean curd with a fine and delicate texture; En Yuan Ju, famous for chaogeda, stir-fried morsel-sized noodle with vegetables and meat; and Yue Sheng Zhai, which prepares wonderful braised beef and lamb.

Beijing also boasts a wide variety of non-Chinese cuisines. Xinjiang cuisine from China's far west has become one of the most popular among Beijing residents, and restaurants serving the dishes of the Uighurs, a Turkic minority from northwest China, are everywhere in Beijing. A typical menu is full of lamb dishes—from tender roast leg of lamb perfectly seasoned with spices, to kabobs, and even sheep's

hearts and intestines, accompanied by heavy bread called nan. A favourite is Xinjiang noodles, long doughy strips cooked with chicken and tomatoes.

For a taste of little-known but delicious Tibetan cuisine without even having to step out of the city, there's always Makye Ame. Here, diners get to sample authentic hot stone dishes; balabani (a mixture of spinach and cheese); tender roasted lamb ribs; beef stir-fried with sour carrots and wrapped in thin, but doughy, pancakes; and roasted mushrooms stuffed with tomatoes and drizzled with garlic and yak butter. The rich cultures and traditions from the Roof of the World are very much alive here, with Tibetan music and dancing; Tibetan waitresses donning traditional attire; and decorative items such as religious paintings, prayer flags and prayer wheels adorning the restaurant.

The year 2006 also saw an invasion of European restaurants and bakeries that have transformed the culinary face of the Chinese capital. Café de la Poste, a French bistro set up by a young French chef, serves excellent steaks. Comptoirs de France, owned by the son of an old French family with its own flourmill, bakes delicious crusty breads and pastries and tarts. W Dine & Wine, Beijing's newest Belgium dining venue opened by Belgian Geoffrey Weckx, a former chef at several five-star hotels in China, presents a variety of moderately priced continental dishes.

A recent trend among restaurants in this highly competitive food market is stylish, contemporary interior design. Minimalism seems to be the guiding design principle at South Silk Road, a restaurant specialising in Yunnan cuisine, and where its dining room doubles as a showroom for artist-owner Fang Lijun's art pieces. Among the popular dishes are tree-bark salad and qiguoji (a clay-pot soup with steamed chicken and tonic herbs). Another of its specialties is homemade sausages seasoned with exotic spices to create a numbing and addictive effect. Niugan jun, wild mushrooms indigenous to Yunnan province, are sautéed with dried chillies and are amazingly tasty.

THIS PAGE (FROM TOP): **An interior view of My Humble House; My Humble House's chic sister restaurant, House by the Park.**

OPPOSITE (FROM TOP): **Fusion cuisine is served at House by the Park; another sophisticated dining area at My Humble House.**

At the other end of the spectrum, unabashed luxury is the name of the game at My Humble House, a chic and sophisticated restaurant that boasts plush leather seats, extravagant interiors, and a bar with gorgeous views of a flower-strewn pool. Its fusion cuisine is equally lavish, with tasty dishes such as crispy cod glazed with a mixture of balsamic vinegar and brown sugar sauce, and accompanied with steamed fresh bamboo and sweet and sour dipping sauce. Another popular dish here is the salsa salad starter, consisting of arugula, red capsicum, tomatoes and thin-sliced braised beef in a unique dressing made of sesame paste and wasabi, with acar (savoury and pungent pickled cucumber) on the side.

Bellagio is another venue where Beijing's beautiful people wine and dine amidst vast, elegant interiors. Here, Sichuanese dishes are given a surprising Taiwanese touch, resulting in house specialties such as gongbao bean curd (gongbao chicken with the meat replaced by humble bean curd), migao (glutinous rice stuffed with dried mushrooms or dried shrimp), or dry fried beef strips cooked with Sichuan peppercorn and dried chillies. Most guests choose to top off their meal with a mountain of Taiwan-style crushed ice, slathered with luxurious toppings of red bean, green bean, passion

fruit, kiwi, mango, strawberry or peanuts, and drizzled with condensed milk. One of these refreshing ices—a good dish for cleansing the palate—can be seen on almost every table.

Lan, undoubtedly one of Beijing's hippest restaurants, may be most appealing for Philippe Starck's surrealistic and eclectic interior design, but its modernistic Sichuan fare is equally good. A popular favourite is huiguo tudou, a play on a traditional dish of pork, vegetable and spicy broad bean sauce, which is cooked twice in the wok; this time, though, the humble potato has taken the place of fatty pork.

At People 8, a loft-type restaurant, diners enter through an almost hidden door, only to find themselves swallowed by the darkness. Just as nervousness starts to set in, staff, who barely stand out in their smart black outfits, come to their rescue. All the food here is served on sleek ceramic dishes and earthy crockery. One of the most innovative items here is spareribs cooked with plums, giving the succulent meat a lovely tart taste.

Shanzhai, a restaurant serving both Chinese and Japanese cuisine, promises guests another out-of-this-world experience. Its sprawling hall, resembling the set of a science fiction movie, has a main dining area with a tall, arched and subtly lit ceiling. On the fringes, standing out from the darkness, somewhat surrealistic, are the sushi counter and teppanyaki section. In the middle of all this, a large ice Buddha statue sits on a lotus under a giant Japanese bell. The translucent, almost glowing Buddha at once appears milky white, then alternates between red, blue, green, yellow and purple. At both ends of the venue are loft-dining areas, with neat tatami mats and natural wooden tables. Each table appears to be even with the floor until the waitress clicks on a remote control and the surface slowly rises several feet into the air so diners can fit their legs beneath. Shanzhai's mission is to provide healthy organic food; its vegetables come from the restaurant's own farm; and detailed records—including the farmer's name—are kept for each piece of vegetable, from planting until it reaches the dining table.

THIS PAGE: Lan, a sophisticated Sichuan restaurant, designed by the famous Philippe Starck.
OPPOSITE: Interior of Lan, with its surreal, 'Alice in Wonderland' use of paintings placed all around the restaurant.

...Starck's surrealistic and eclectic interior design...

chaoyang

> The World of Suzie Wong
> Torana Gallery
> Rechenberg

Liufang

Liangmaqiao Road

North Nongzhanguan Road

Chaoyang Park

Dongzhimen

Dongzhimen

Xindong Road

North Third Ring Road

Chaoyang Park Road

> Bayhood No.9
> The Dining Room
> GREEN T. HOUSE Living
> The Orchard
> Zenspa

Olympic Green

Beijing 798 Art Zone

Dongsishitiao

Sanlitun Road

North Gongti Road

South Nongzhanguan Road

South Chaoyang Park Road

Dongzhimen Avenue

Workers' Gymnasium

Workers' Stadium

Panjiayuan Market

Beijing Amusement Park

Chaoyangmen

South Gongti Road

Dongyue Temple

Tuanjiehu Park

> GREEN T. HOUSE
> Face
> Kerry Centre Hotel
> Centro Bar + Lounge

0 km 1 2 3 4 km

Chaoyangmenwai Avenue

Northeast Third Ring Road

Chaoyang Road

North Ritan Road

Dongdaqiao Road

Ritan Park

Guanghua Road

> Hatsune
> Kagen
> House By The Park

> Cottage Boutique
> St Regis Hotel
> St Regis Spa + Club
> Danieli's
> China World Hotel

Ritan Road

Embassy District

Silk Street Market

Jianguomenwai Avenue

Guomao

Jianguo Road

Ancient Observatory

Jianguomen

Yonganli

Park Hyatt Beijing
Ascott Beijing

Dawanglu

ingzhan

Beijing Railway Station

N

Legend

✈	Airport
	Expressway
	Urban ring road
	Main road
	Other road
	Railway
	Railway station
	Light rail
	Subway
○	Subway/light rail station
◯	Water

Beijing East Railway Station

0 km 0.25 0.5 0.75 1 km

a city on the move

The layout of Beijing looks like a lake into which a stone has been thrown, sending concentric ripples spreading outwards. These are a series of ring roads that circle the centre of the city, getting increasingly larger as they move outside, with Chang'an Avenue, the Avenue of Eternal Peace, cutting across the centre from east to west, and dividing north and south.

Beijing is a city on the move. Construction is devouring vast swatches of the city in the run-up to the 2008 Olympics, unfortunately sometimes resulting in the destruction of old hutong (alleyways) and traditional courtyard homes, and throwing up in their place various modern structures. The debate rages on about the wisdom of this makeover, and the capital today faces the challenge of promoting economic development and modernisation without completely erasing the charm of the old city.

The city is a jumble of unique neighbourhoods. It's divided into 18 municipal and suburban districts, but just six of these are really urban and thus a magnet for visitors. Dongcheng (East District) encompasses the Forbidden City, Tiananmen Square and other historical attractions. Xicheng (West District) includes idyllic Beihai Park, temples, and a series of lakes fringed by willow trees and hutong-lined courtyards. The southern districts include Chongwen in the southeast and Xuanwu in the southwest, which contain some of the city's oldest neighbourhoods, with a history of folk arts, including opera, acrobatics and storytelling. Chongwen is also home to some of Beijing's most famous laozihao (old brand name shops). Haidian, the bustling technology and university district northwest of the Third Ring Road, is packed with student hangouts, bookstores, high-tech firms and electronics shops. Chaoyang is the biggest and busiest district, occupying the areas north, east, and south of the eastern Second Ring Road. As this district is located outside the old city walls, there are few traces of old China.

THIS PAGE: With the 2008 Olympics in the horizon, Beijing is undergoing a massive makeover like never before.

OPPOSITE: One of the many new glassy skyscrapers lining the Central Business District.

PAGE 52: The National Stadium in northern Beijing, dubbed the 'Bird's Nest', is one of several venues to be built from scratch for the 2008 Olympics.

ritan park

Ritan Park, also known as the Sun Altar Park, is the place to see old and new China rubbing shoulders. One of Beijing's oldest parks, Ritan was built in 1530, and in imperial times it included a large raised circular altar for imperial sacrifices to the sun. Today, only the foundation remains, and this once holy space has been taken over by

children riding bicycles, mothers and daughters playing badminton, and ageing kite aficionados holding long reels of string, squinting to see their 'centipedes' flying in the distance, now just specks in the sky.

In the morning, the park is full of people practising the pastimes of past and present—moving sometimes gracefully, sometimes not—between the ancient Chinese architecture that can still be found scattered around the park. In one corner, a group of elderly men and women go through the slow paces of a taiqi routine, while a few feet away another group practises the faster movements of traditional swordfighting and martial arts. Opposite them, a boom box blasts loud disco music as several middle-aged women (and the odd middle-aged man) mimic their teacher's moves. Despite all the surrounding distractions, just a few yards away, some couples are lost in their own world, completely absorbed in an elaborate ballroom dance. In the distance, one can hear the cacophonous sound of a Chinese stringed instrument accompanying the shrill, high-pitched voice of an amateur Peking opera singer.

It should come as no surprise that the park has also become a busy sea of commerce as enterprising entrepreneurs seek to exploit its natural resources to turn a quick yuan. There are several restaurants, including Xiheyaju, which serves Cantonese and Sichuanese fare on the northwest corner; Xiao Wangfu's home-style cooking near the north gate; and La Galleria, just west of the south gate, which serves decent dim sum amidst views of the park. In addition, there's a yoga studio, rock climbing wall, miniature golf course, and a playground with bumper cars. In the warmer months, the Stone Boat Café, a cosy coffee-shop-cum-bar situated beside a small lake, stages outdoor world music performances, from American rock to gigs by a small Indian-Western quartet to Uighur folk music from China's far northwest. In between all of this action, which goes on non-stop from 6 a.m. to 10 p.m., one can find semi-hidden pockets of green solitude or a few quiet benches for a bit of relaxation.

THIS PAGE (FROM TOP): Reflections of Beijingers as they practise taiqi, or shadow boxing; a woman plays with a diabolo in front of an imperial structure.

OPPOSITE: Honing the ancient art of martial swordfighting in Ritan Park, a popular venue for daily exercises among local residents.

dongyue temple

Dongyue Temple, one of Beijing's most colourful temples, was built between 1314 and 1320. Once one of the biggest and oldest Taoist temples in Beijing, the structure was destroyed by fire, and was later rebuilt during the Ming Dynasty. Although the present temple complex was constructed in the Qing Dynasty, there are still traces of its colourful past. The complex has hundreds of life-size plaster figures, including statues of the God of Taishan and his senior aides in the Hall of Taishan (one of China's five sacred Taoist mountains). A more macabre scene awaits along the temple corridors: 72 statues of 'chiefs of departments' handing out horrifying punishments to sinners suffering in the 18 Layers of Hell—a sort of Dante's *Inferno* with Chinese characteristics.

Dongyue Temple is a wonderful place to visit during Chinese New Year to sample one of Beijing's more genuine and interesting temple fairs. At that time, the old temple is full of stilt walkers—heavily made-up young children walking on long stilts—and people selling old folk crafts and traditional Beijing snacks. One can easily spend an entire day here just soaking in the festive atmosphere.

bustling bazaars

Once a bustling outdoor market, the old Silk Alley has now moved indoors into a multi-storey building and been renamed the Silk Street Market. It's still packed with bargain-hunting tourists and purveyors of pirated brand-name goods, including Rolex watches and Prada bags. However, Panjiayuan Market, located slightly further south on a former building site, is the place for those seeking a more authentic bazaar atmosphere.

Visitors could be forgiven for being a bit taken aback when they first arrive at the Panjiayuan Market, which looks more like a ruin than China's premier weekly garage sale. But once they step beyond the crumbling walls surrounding this nondescript dirt lot, they come upon a whole new world. Panjiayuan Market has a Qing Dynasty atmosphere. Before the first rays of morning light begin to spread over the city, a constant chatter of bargaining can already be heard rippling across the lot as serious

THIS PAGE (FROM TOP): Seemingly endless rows of knick-knacks and handicraft at the city's popular Panjiayuan Market; a large incense coil at Dongyue Temple, one of Beijing's biggest and oldest Taoist temples.
OPPOSITE: A hawker takes a break in front of a 'wall' of colourful Chinese traditional lanterns at Beijing's Panjiayuan Market.

Panjiayuan Market has a Qing Dynasty atmosphere.

buyers come early to haggle with the hundreds of peddlers, whose accents betray origins from all corners of China. It will be a few more hours before the amateurs—who are more interested in knick-knacks and handicrafts—begin to arrive on the scene, by which time, apparently, most of the market's real bargains will have been snapped up.

Just inside the entrance is a line of food stalls, where cooks turn over mountains of noodles on large frying pans. There are stacks of scallion pancakes and bubbling vats—contents unknown. While buyers take a break from the haggling to wolf down a quick breakfast, food hawkers go on the offensive, charging into the crowd, holding large pans of food high over their heads.

The range of products, spread out on plastic sheets on the ground, is amazing. Yes, one will find the same factory-fresh snuff bottles, porcelain and traditional paintings that can be found in souvenir shops all over the city. But this is not what attracts the thousands who flock here each week.

The real attractions are the odd pieces one might find peppered among the instant antiques. Many of these have apparently been gathered from all over China. There are large stone temple lions, Chinese bows, a huge traditional wooden door with brass fittings (supposedly Ming Dynasty), a windup

THIS PAGE (FROM TOP): Paintings with revolutionary themes on sale at the Panjiayuan Market; decked appropriately in a blue Mao outfit and cap, a stall owner sells 'Maomorabilia' to locals and tourists allike.

OPPOSITE: In recent years, China has experienced a nostalgic interest in artefacts from the Cultural Revolution.

Columbia gramophone, old temple roof tiles, and a Qing Dynasty leather horse saddle with fine metal trim. On one visit, one may find old lanterns, the wire frame rusted, the fine red paper faded. On the next, one may stumble upon wooden grain boxes, the wood worn smooth from long use.

The market also has a large collection of Mao memorabilia, including Mao buttons made from a wide assortment of materials, Mao busts, Chairman Mao's Little Red Book, and copies of old books and magazines featuring the Great Helmsman and other top leaders on their covers.

Some of the best finds are pop-art items from the Cultural Revolution (1966–76). A smiling Red Guard on the face of an alarm clock waves Mao's Little Red Book as the second hand makes its way around the clock face; elsewhere are ballerina statues from revolutionary ballets and porcelain wall tiles depicting scenes from famous revolutionary plays. A statue, painted in a dull glaze, shows a worker, a farmer and a soldier standing shoulder to shoulder, the tools of their trade—hammer, sickle and rifle—held high in the air. There are also faded Red Guard armbands with Chinese characters painted in bright yellow, and a large assortment of posters, showing fierce-looking soldiers, peasants smiling in the fields, or factory workers grinning as they toil away.

From the large amounts of such goods found scattered among the sellers, there appears to be a whole new industry which has sprung up to produce all of the above items. Admittedly, their authenticity is debatable, yet from the fairly reasonable prices, you cannot really get cheated.

...this is a great place to see some of the cooler aspects of Chinese culture.

beijing 798 art zone

The Beijing 798 Art Zone, also known as the Dashanzi Art District or the 798 Factory, is located in an old factory complex now full of galleries, nightlife spots, and Timezone 8, an excellent English-language art bookstore. Contemporary art exhibitions—from paintings to performance art to ceramics and sculpture—are held here regularly. Whether or not you love art, this is a great place to see some of the cooler aspects of Chinese culture. It's best to go to Dashanzi Art District on a late weekend afternoon, when you can take

your time to browse the galleries until it gets dark, and then spend the rest of the evening at one of its hip restaurants or coffee shops.

Way back in 1953, the East Germans had helped to build this complex of Bauhaus-style factories, but the ailing state-run factories abandoned their spaces when business turned down in 2001. Lured by low rents and large open spaces with abundant natural light, several Beijing artists raced in to fill the gap. Businessmen arrived on the heels of the artists, setting up coffee shops and Western and Chinese restaurants.

THIS PAGE (FROM TOP): Relaxing in a coffee shop that adjoins the Timezone 8 bookstore; a glass-enclosed gallery; a Mao jacket as art.
OPPOSITE: Sculptures inspired by Emperor Qin Shi Huang's terracotta army on display at the Beijing 798 Art Zone. They are the work of Norwegian artist Marian Heyerdahl.

central business district

Chaoyang, a sprawling area, is home to everyday Chinese who live in government housing, the new middle class residing in modern high-rise apartments, multinational corporations, pleasant-looking foreign embassies, five-star international hotels, and the Central Business District, which includes the China World Trade Center and a bevy of fast-rising shiny, new commercial complexes.

Some critics have remarked that Beijing's broad layout—marked by its wide boulevards and streets—lacks the feeling of intimacy found in other world cities, which are more amenable to pedestrians. The new Central Business District is attempting to correct this shortcoming of older

sections of the city by creating new forms of urban living with areas in which people can live, work, mingle, dine, shop, or simply walk around more easily.

The jewel in the crown of Beijing's newly rising Central Business District is the grand and impressive Beijing Yintai Centre, a sprawling complex which includes the Park Hyatt Beijing, a 63-storey, 237-room boutique hotel, condominium residence, and retail mall flanked by two office buildings. From the hotel's rooftop bar, designed to resemble a Chinese lantern, diners can enjoy spectacular views of the city.

Nearby, the China World Trade Center is building its third phase of office and commercial space. Opposite this stands Jianwai SOHO, one of the biggest commercial projects in Beijing, which was developed by husband and wife team Pan Shiyi and Zhang Xin, and designed by one of Japan's top architects, Riken Yamamoto. Blending residential and commercial living, while adhering to the philosophy that 'small is beautiful', Jianwai SOHO is unlike other similar but older complexes in Beijing; with no walls or gates enclosing it, it appears entirely open to the rest of the Central Business District, and yet, pedestrians entering the complex will have the impression that they are stepping into a self-contained micro-city. For one, vehicles are either confined to the edges of the complex or must enter through a subterranean passageway leading up to the lower levels of the buildings. Inside, parks, shops and restaurants line the ground level, while several layers of gardens exist on the buildings' lower levels, providing residents and visitors with a bit of refreshing greenery.

An array of other innovative—and often controversial—architectural projects have already been completed or are in the works around the city. Several of these are designed by internationally known architects. One prime example is the new CCTV Tower. The multi-million-dollar complex, designed by Dutch architect Rem Koolhaas, will employ a continuous loop of horizontal and vertical sections, and is set to be the tallest skyscraper in Beijing. Given the city's accelerated growth and rapidly changing urbanscape, however, it may not be too farfetched to surmise that several other buildings still on the drawing board could soon climb past it.

The new Central Business District is trying to correct this shortcoming of older sections of the city...

2008 olympics

China will host the Olympics in 2008 and many of the leading venues are located in the Chaoyang district. An estimated 2.5 million visitors and some 30,000 journalists will visit Beijing in 2008, and the government is determined to make this 'the best games ever'. The Communist Party, known for its efficiency in getting things done when reputation is at stake, worked so fast to finish Olympic structures that the International Olympic Committee had to ask them to slow down. They were concerned that the sporting venues would lose some of their glitter before the opening ceremony.

Many of the projects have been designed by top-notch international architects, and they are impressive. Twelve brand-new Olympic venues are being built from scratch,

with another 11 existing ones being renovated. A consortium led by Swiss-based Herzog & de Meuron Architekten of Switzerland is constructing the RMB3.8 billion (US$500 million) main arena for the Olympic Games. Dubbed the 'Bird's Nest', the space-age looking National Stadium is made of interlocking bands of grey steel covered with a transparent membrane and a retractable roof, and will seat close to 100,000 spectators. An Australian-Chinese consortium headed by PTW Architects Australia is building the RMB757 million (US$100 million) National Aquatics Center, dubbed the 'Watercube'.

But the Olympics are more than just high-tech concrete and steel structures. The Olympic mascots, cartoon figures known as the 'Five Friendlies', are on sale throughout the country, with Olympic watchdogs determined to keep them out of pirates' stands at the Silk Street Market. According to the Olympics website, the five mascots embody the natural characteristics of four of China's most popular animals—the fish, panda, Tibetan antelope, and swallow—and the Olympic flame.

Meanwhile, the government is trying to deal with a potential problem: the weather. Officials are hard at work on a project that they say could delay or push away rain clouds that might disrupt the Games. What may prove to be much more difficult, however, is changing people's behaviour, another stated goal of the Olympic organisers. The city's Communist Party secretary has promised to 're-educate' people who use locally invented profanity to cheer and jeer players at sporting events. To raise Beijing's 'civility' level, the government will crack down on people who use jingma, a Chinese phrase loosely translated as 'Beijing cursing'.

According to the Chinese media, a big push is being made to discourage the habit of spitting, which is widespread throughout China. Millions of brochures, along with paper sanitary bags with the Chinese symbol for 'mucus' on them, are being distributed to convince citizens that the habit is unhygienic. Anyone found expectorating on the sidewalk would either have to clean up after himself or cough up a RMB50 (US$7) fine.

THIS PAGE (FROM TOP): The state-of-the-art plastic surface of China's National Aquatics Center reacts to lighting and projection, creating visual and sensory effects as it alternates between transparency and translucency; children mesmerised by a shadow puppet show featuring the five Olympic mascots.

OPPOSITE: A very young member of China's national gymnastics team goes through her paces, encouraged by the framed photos of former champions.

nightlife

Beijing is now ramming its way into the 21st century after decades of staid Marxism and Maoism. Young people in the city are excitedly embracing China's latest 'ism'— me-ism—and the hopping bars and clubs in Chaoyang are the new temples to this religion. The booming bar scene is just another reflection of the changes that are going on throughout the city as it prepares to host the 2008 Olympics.

The World of Suzie Wong, on the crowded bar and restaurant strip beside Chaoyang Park's west gate, is named after the 1950s novel and 1960 movie starring Nancy Kwan and William Holden. The hip hangout charms with two floors of antiques and porcelain, carved wooden doors, and even a cauldron filled with rose petals.

THIS PAGE (FROM TOP): A clubber is bathed in blue light at one of Beijing's growing number of popular nightspots; a guitarist jumps on a bar stage—Beijing has the best live music scene in all of China.

OPPOSITE: An excited weekend crowd at Babyface, one of the capital's hottest clubs.

On West Gongti Road, flashy clubs with names like Babyface, Cargo, Coco Banana and Angel are packed with beautiful Beijing women—movie stars, models, singers and artists—and rich businessmen, as evidenced by the parking lot full of luxury cars. Inside, imported deejays spin vinyl recordings. At the north gate of the Workers' Stadium and nearby Sanlitun Road, a continuous stream of Beijing hipsters enters, as if led in a trance by the hip hop and R&B music throbbing from several bars (which have displaced venues once devoted to basketball courts and ping-pong tables).

At Mix, it's wall-to-wall people drinking, dancing, or lost in conversation. The crowd runs the gamut of contemporary Beijing society: Chinese university students, diplomats, well-heeled business types, expatriate suits, Mongolian prostitutes, and foreign language students. The hip hop crowd, with their baggy jeans and shirts, prowls the side of the dance floor, while the more stylish 20-somethings sit at the tables, affecting boredom. On the second floor, young foreign businessmen stare down in amusement at the dance floor, which has suddenly become engulfed in a steamy mist, followed by bubbles, which in turn are replaced by falling confetti. Behind the bar, the waiters do tricks with fire.

Welcome to the New China.

Young people in the city are excitedly embracing China's latest 'ism'—me-ism...

ascott beijing

...luxurious living in China's vast capital...

THIS PAGE: *The warm, welcoming reception lobby at Ascott Beijing.*

OPPOSITE (FROM TOP): *At Somerset Grand Fortune Garden, also run by Ascott International, service and guest welfare is paramount; the modern setting of Somerset ZhongGuanCun, part of the Ascott International group of accommodations, well reflects the busy capital city of Beijing.*

Combining personalised service with the facilities and space that define luxurious living in China's vast capital, Ascott Beijing serviced apartments offer a welcome alternative to the numerous five-star hotels available in the city. Rated first in the Top 100 Serviced Residences rankings for four consecutive years, the deluxe apartments offer much more than a place to stay. Designer furniture, state-of-the-art technology and excellent amenities ensure all the comforts of the finest luxury hotels with the self-containment and proprietary sense of one's own space.

Located in the heart of Beijing's business and retail district along Jianguomenwai Avenue, Ascott Beijing is within walking distance of a host of offices, shops, restaurants and sightseeing attractions. Nearby, Oriental Plaza is home to Beijing's largest shopping mall and some of the city's most prestigious office space. Workers' Stadium, which has long been a magnet for the

city's hottest restaurants, is a gentle evening stroll away, mere minutes by taxi. Tiananmen Square, The Forbidden City, Temple of Heaven, Chaoyang Park and Beijing Railway Station are all also within a convenient distance. For anything further afield, Ascott Beijing thoughtfully provides a limousine service, facilitating access to any part of town.

The spacious apartments cater to business travellers and long-term residents. With options that range from one- to four-bedrooms, both single businessmen and large families can enjoy the luxury accommodation. Interiors are simple and elegant, using predominantly light colours to convey brightness and freshness. Asian artwork and Chinese screens add a bold Oriental touch to neutral backgrounds. Pale fabrics, wood furniture and state-of-the-art technologies set a modern and sophisticated tone. A kitchen with fully fitted stainless steel accessories includes a six gas-ring oven, a washing machine, dryer and microwave. A hatch through to the living and dining area allows light to flood across the work surfaces and is an indication of the strong sense of fun and inventiveness that permeates the design. The ensuite marble bathrooms, equipped with a deep-soaking tub and separate rain-shower, are separated from the bedrooms by a glass panel. Satellite television and DVD players form an impressive home entertainment unit

THIS PAGE: *Enjoy a cool swim in the indoor pool to relax and unwind.*

OPPOSITE (CLOCKWISE FROM TOP): *Ascott Beijing's modern gym facilities; a long, hot sauna is the perfect antidote to a full day in the city; the height of luxurious living in the very heart of China's capital; the well-equipped meeting rooms are ideal for business travellers.*

that can be enjoyed from the living area and the bedroom. With such creature comforts on hand, a night in at Ascott Beijng can be considered to be on par with a night out in China's dazzling capital. A daily-maid service, laundry and dry-cleaning services, and home delivery from the on-site mini-mart allow guests to avoid the hassle of domestic chores.

Further relaxation can be found within the abundant facilities. Flooded with light from a glass roof and surrounded by palm trees, the indoor pool emits a warm and inviting glow. A jacuzzi, steam room and sauna with a relaxation area ensure the perfect wind down after a day of meetings or sightseeing. The Health Club also features a fully equipped gym with personal television screens and an aerobics studio. Families residing at Ascott Beijing can make use of the separate children's pool and the 24-hour baby-sitting service. Businessmen

have access to high-speed Internet connection throughout the building and a business centre with secretarial support. Three restaurants, serving Asian and western cuisine, are located within the building for those who fancy a quiet meal in its luxurious confines.

Ascott International also runs Somerset Grand Fortune Garden, Beijing and Somerset ZhongGuanCun serviced apartments. The combined 375 luxury residences feature similar facilities found at Ascott Beijing, with fully equipped kitchens, home entertainment systems and contemporary settings. At each, an indoor pool, sauna and health centre offer a calming respite from the city outside. A breakfast lounge and meal delivery service provide for the occasional night off, while a wireless Internet connection within the apartments and a fully serviced business centre keep guests connected.

Close to the numerous restaurants and bars around Sanlitun, Somerset Grand Fortune Garden is located in the 3rd Embassy District, within walking distance of the Lufthansa Centre and its surrounding offices. Somerset ZhongGuanCun can be found in the heart of Beijing's high technology zone in Haidian District, 15 minutes' walk to the new Beijing Olympic Village.

ROOMS
310

FOOD
Casa Mia: Italian • Subway: sandwich delicatessen • Sui Gao: Japanese • Sentosa UE: Singaporean and Thai • Xiang Ji Yan Chi Bao: Chinese

DRINK
Starbucks • Yang Yue Lou Teahouse

FEATURES
indoor pool • jacuzzi • sauna • dance studio • steam room • business centre • high-speed Internet access • limousine service • mini-mart • retail and service shops • concierge service • event and function rooms • gym

NEARBY
China World Trade Center • Silk Street Market • Forbidden City • Tiananmen Square • Ritan Park • Temple of Heaven

CONTACT
108B Jianguo Road
Chaoyang District, Beijing 100022 •
telephone: +86.10.6567 8100 •
facsimile: +86.10.6567 8122 •
email: enquiry.china@the-ascott.com •
website: www.the-ascott.com

bayhood no. 9

...rolling hills, pine forests and lakes.

THIS PAGE (CLOCKWISE FROM ABOVE):
With the rapid rise in affluence, golf is getting more and more popular in mainland China; players can practise at night in comfort at the driving range; luxurious rooms to relax in after a full 18-hole game.

OPPOSITE (CLOCKWISE FROM TOP):
Elegant décor at the Clubhouse; visitors can check out the latest golf outfits at the boutique; a spectacular view from the Clubhouse rooftop terrace.

Located a short 30 minutes' drive from central Beijing, Bayhood No. 9 is an exclusive premier golf club and resort which covers 133 hectares (329 acres) of rolling hills, pine forests and lakes. Beihu, which is the area surrounding the club, has a rich history dating back more than 600 years. During the Ming Dynasty, it was used as the imperial hunting grounds and was also the site of one of the four imperial gardens situated outside the capital.

Designed by award-winning Canadian firm Nelson and Haworth Golf Course Architects, Bayhood No. 9 offers a beautiful 18-hole course covering 80 hectares (198 acres), two practice greens, a 9-hole night-time course, a driving range and a state-of-the-art Clubhouse.

Not for the faint-hearted, Bayhood No. 9's signature hole comes after 17 challenging holes in a tranquil setting. The 18th hole is set in an amphitheatre of mounds and trees as well as a lake which is strategically guarded by a bunker. The water lies at the edge of the small undulating green of the finishing hole, near the world-class Clubhouse and spa. Bent grass, which is known for its lush green colour, is used for the putting greens while Kentucky grass is used for the fairways.

The driving range which covers 10 hectares (25 acres) has fully equipped short game facilities which adhere to United States Golf Association (USGA) standards. The 40 driving stations and 22 private rooms with double-bay driving stations are also available for rental. Travellers can also enjoy amenities such as high-definition television screens, high-speed Internet connection, shower rooms and dining areas.

In March 2007, Bayhood No. 9 opened the first and only British Professional Golfers' Association (PGA)-branded golf academy in Asia, which offers the latest technology in golf analysis covering all major aspects of the golf swing and game. This means a team of certified golf instructors from the PGA-managed St Andrews Links Golf Academy is at hand to provide coaching programmes customised according to the members' skills.

The Clubhouse at Bayhood No. 9 offers a beautiful setting to enjoy a deserved drink at the 18th hole. At The Dining Room, some 18 private dining rooms serve delicious traditional Cantonese cuisine to members and non-members alike. Plans are also underway to open a boutique hotel with private villas, conference facilities, a luxurious spa and a fitness centre.

ROOMS
100

FOOD
The Dining Room: Cantonese fusion

DRINK
bar

FEATURES
18-hole golf course • 9-hole night-time course • 2 practice greens • driving range • PGA golf academy • massage suites • Clubhouse • sauna

NEARBY
Summer Palace • Great Wall (Badaling section) • Ming Tombs

CONTACT
9 Anwai Beihu, Chaoyang District, Beijing 100012 •
telephone: +86.10.6491 9797 •
facsimile: +86.10.6491 8888 •
email: info@bayhood9.com •
website: www.bayhood9.com

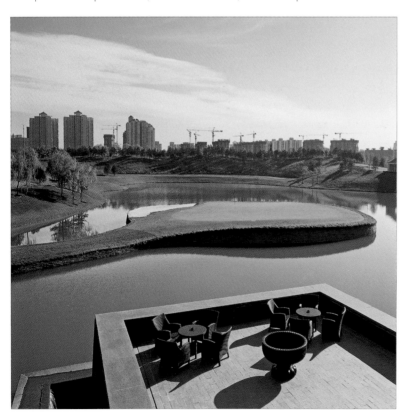

china world hotel

...the possibilities seem endless...

THIS PAGE (FROM BOTTOM): *The grand lobby of China World Hotel; the luxurious bedroom of one of the Beijing Suites, in a lush palette of soothing earth tones.*

OPPOSITE (CLOCKWISE FROM CENTRE): *The stunning wall mural in the hotel lobby, etched in fine gold paint; expect events hosted at China World Hotel to be perfect down to the very last, intricate detail; dine in greatest comfort at Aria, the hotel's signature restaurant.*

Located within the prestigious China World Trade Center, Shangri-La's China World Hotel is one of Beijing's finest. Its excellent location means that some of the best shopping in the city is at its doorstep, from Chinese antiques to high-end designer boutiques. Guests also enjoy close proximity to Beijing's most magnificent sights, including the Forbidden City, the Temple of Heaven and Tiananmen Square.

Renovated at a cost of US$30 million in 2003, this swish hotel is all marble floors with rich gold accents. In its guestrooms, sumptuous furnishings in soothing shades of cream complement the views of the city below. Comfort, luxury and style define the 716 rooms, each appointed with sleek wall panels and contemporary Asian art. The hotel's Premier Rooms offer 55 sq m (600 sq ft) of elegance with spacious living rooms, dressing areas and bathrooms. For more discerning travellers, the Horizon Club on the hotel's top four floors offers added perks including exclusive use of the Club Lounge and 24-hour butler service.

In keeping with their innovative brand of service, China World Hotel was the first in Beijing to offer an airport butler service. These butlers take care of guests' airport formalities from the moment they leave their flight to when they get on board again at the end of their trip.

Dining is an equally special experience, with a myriad of restaurants and bars to choose from. The hotel's signature restaurant, Aria, serves what is regarded as the city's finest modern European cuisine. Downstairs at Aria Bar, guests enjoy jazz music and sample a range of wines and cocktails. At Scene a Café, guests love to sit with a view of the open kitchens and watch the chefs as they deftly prepare meals for a buffet of Asian and international favourites. Those in search of authentic Chinese can head off to Summer Palace, which serves Cantonese and Beijing specialities. Meanwhile, at Nadaman, guests can dine on authentic Japanese. For a touch of the majestic, head to the Lobby Lounge, with its imperial Chinese palace design and where a full orchestra performs live on weekends during afternoon high tea.

A state-of-the-art fitness centre is open to all guests, while indoor tennis courts, a squash court and a heated indoor pool provide for all needs. Those in search of more languorous pleasures can indulge in a steam bath or order up a massage. Indeed, the possibilities seem endless.

ROOMS
716

FOOD
Summer Palace: Chinese • Lobby Lounge: high teas • Aria: modern European • Nadaman: Japanese • Scene a Café: international

DRINK
Aria • Lobby Lounge

FEATURES
indoor pool • squash court • tennis courts • gym • jacuzzi • high-speed Internet access • business centre • airport butler service

NEARBY
Forbidden City • China World Trade Center • China World Shopping Mall • Silk Street Market • Great Hall of the People

CONTACT
1 Jianguomenwai Avenue Chaoyang District, Beijing 100004 • telephone: +86.10.6505 2266 • facsimile: +86.10.6505 0828 • email: cwh@shangri-la.com •

kerry centre hotel

...situated in the heart of the business district and close to embassies...

THIS PAGE: *All guestrooms are fitted with high-speed Internet access.*

OPPOSITE (CLOCKWISE FROM TOP): *Centro—the hotel's award-winning 24-hour bar; the Kerry Centre Hotel is the fourth addition to The Shangri-La Hotels and Resorts' family of hotels in Beijing; delectable cuisine at The Horizon Chinese Restaurant; after workouts, visitors can luxuriate at the hotel's spa.*

The hip and contemporary Kerry Centre Hotel is situated in the heart of the business district and close to embassies, and some of the city's best sightseeing spots which include the Silk Street Market and Ritan Park. Within five years of its opening in 1999, the hotel has already received numerous accolades, including the prestigious Five-Star Diamond Award from the American Academy of Hospitality Sciences in 2003 and 2004. It was also voted one of the Top Five Hotels in Beijing by *Euromoney* in 2001.

Designed and furnished like a swish, modern home, its rooms are equipped with four-pipe temperature control and an ergonomically designed executive desk. Travellers staying in the Horizon Club rooms can enjoy benefits including the 24-hour butler service, suit pressing, an in-room fax machine and scanner, complimentary high-speed Internet access and use of the Club's plush meeting room. Evening cocktails are available every night at the Horizon Club lounge.

ROOMS
487

FOOD
The Horizon Chinese Restaurant: Cantonese and Sichuan • Coffee Garden: international • Bento and Berries: delicatessen

DRINK
Centro Bar and Lounge

FEATURES
sauna • jacuzzi • health club • indoor tennis courts • squash courts • outdoor jogging and roller-blading track • high-speed Internet access

NEARBY
Silk Street Market • Ritan Park • Tuanjiehu Park

CONTACT
1 Guanghua Road
Chaoyang District, Beijing 100020 •
telephone: +86.10.6561 8833 •
facsimile: +86.10.6561 2626 •
email: hbkc@shangri-la.com •
website: www.shangri-la.com

Sprawled across three floors and 6,000 sq m (64,560 sq ft), Kerry Sports impresses with state-of-the-art facilities that include a gym with an extensive array of professional exercise equipment. Visitors can also relax in the five-lane 35-m (115-ft) indoor pool which comes complete with jacuzzis, a heated indoor pool, and a plunge pool for children. A haven for fitness enthusiasts, Kerry Sports is equipped with squash courts, indoor tennis courts, and a recreation room for billiards, snooker and table tennis. A multi-function court which incorporates an NBA-compliant basketball court can also double up as badminton courts, with a spectator seating capacity of 100.

As the hotel's signature restaurant, The Horizon Chinese Restaurant serves authentic Cantonese, Sichuan and other regional cuisine, ranging from delicate portions of dim sum to magnificent banquets. Centro Bar and Lounge is open 24 hours a day and offers cocktails, fine wines, live music and is suitable for breakfast meetings, happy hour drinks or late night entertaining.

park hyatt beijing

...luxury, gracious service and spectacular views with the convenience of a central location.

THIS PAGE: *Rooms at Park Hyatt Beijing exude luxury with soft lighting and shades of cream.*

OPPOSITE (FROM TOP): *Sleek graphic touches add a stylish air to the Park Hyatt Beijing guestrooms; the Beijing Yintai Centre lights up the Central Business District; full-height windows offer views over the very heart of the city.*

Lighting up the Central Business District, the gleaming new towers of the Beijing Yintai Centre, opening in early 2008, are an impressive reflection of the city's increasingly luxurious and glamorous façade. Occupying the top floors of the main Park Tower is a new addition to China's influx of luxury brands, the Park Hyatt Beijing, and with it some of the city's most exclusive accommodation and unique dining and entertainment venues. The tower is crowned with a Chinese palace 'lantern' at its apex, which at night lights up like an iconic beacon.

Located directly opposite the China World Trade Center along the famed Chang'an Avenue and a mere 15 minutes away from Forbbiden City, Park Hyatt Beijing combines contemporary luxury, gracious service and spectacular views with the convenience of a central location. Sophisticated, stylish and ultra-modern in design, the new hotel is both visually stunning and exceptionally equipped with an impressive range of facilities and amenities.

On arrival, express elevators sweep guests up to Level 63 where the sky lobby and lounge are located. Guestrooms and suites, which range from 45 sq m (480 sq ft) to 240 sq m (2,600 sq ft) in size, are thoughtfully provided with every comfort, including a flat-screen television, DVD player, high-speed wireless Internet connection, personal safe with laptop charger and a coffee press supplied with freshly ground coffee. With a fresh cup of steaming aromatic java in hand, guests can further indulge themselves in the spacious spa-inspired bathrooms where a luxuriating deep-soaking bathtub and separate shower with a powerful, oversized rainforest showerhead will invigorate even the weariest of travel-jaded souls.

A health club on Level 6 and an exclusive spa featuring eight treatment rooms on Levels 59 and 60 offer an enticing menu of calming massages, cleansing body wraps and rejuvenating scrubs. Both facilities boast an exercise studio and a 25-m (82-ft) indoor swimming pool.

With 360° views of the sparkling night cityscape, Park Hyatt is home to Beijing's highest restaurant. On the top floor, a speciality restaurant serves international cuisine in an outdoor garden terrace environment with a soaring glass pyramid ceiling. Below it, the bar's dazzling views, live jazz and delicious cocktails ensure an inspiring evening. For something a little more intimate, private dining suites offer fine Cantonese cuisine with personal butler service.

For leisure, visitors can enjoy a sprawling entertainment zone featuring three bars, wine cellars and live music, topped with an expansive roof garden with lush landscaping, stone-paved terraces and myriad water features. Guests can also cater to their every possible whim and discover the latest trends from fashion capitals at the concept stores in Park Life.

Created by a team of leading architects and designers including the award-winning American architectural firm John Portman & Associates, the centre fuses natural elements and materials to offer a calming and residential atmosphere. Water features and greenery dominate the open public spaces, making the whole complex a veritable 'urban oasis' where people can live, work, shop, dine and entertain in a single location.

ROOMS
237

FOOD
speciality restaurant: international • lobby lounge: Western and Chinese • private dining: Cantonese • trattoria

DRINK
bar • entertainment centre

FEATURES
health club • spa • high-speed Internet access • indoor pools • outdoor terrace and garden • Park Life shopping • meeting suites • ballroom • business suites • residential-style event facility • parking facilities

NEARBY
China World Trade Center • Embassy District • Silk Street Market

CONTACT
2 Jianguomenwai Avenue
Chaoyang District, Beijing 100022 •
telephone: +86.10.8567 1234 •
facsimile: +86.10.8567 1000 •
email: parkhyattbeijing@hyattintl.com •
website: beijing.park.hyatt.com

st regis hotel

...reflects the luxury and traditions of a bygone era.

THIS PAGE (CLOCKWISE FROM BOTTOM):
Astor Grill entices epicureans with its steaks and seafood; imposing columns add to the opulent atmosphere at the Club Wing Lobby; diners can have a veritable feast at Celestial Court.

OPPOSITE (CLOCKWISE FROM TOP): *The Garden Lounge is an ideal venue for evening relaxation; visitors can store their personal favourite choices at the Cigar Lounge's specially designed in-house humidor cabinet; the luxuriousness of the Diplomat Deluxe room ensures a memorable stay.*

Located in the centre of Beijing's business, shopping and diplomatic district, St Regis Hotel reflects the luxury and traditions of a bygone era. Just a few minutes' walk away from renowned sightseeing spots of Ritan Park and Silk Street Market, St Regis is right next to the historic Beijing International Club, a famed meeting place for government officials, foreign dignitaries and international correspondents.

In the main lobby, the elegant décor is accentuated with intricately designed Chinese chests, a warm glow created by lacquer lamps, and a huge gilded mirror framed above the large fireplace. This opulent, traditional atmosphere has not gone unnoticed; in 2006, the hotel was ranked second in *Condé Nast Traveller's* 'Best Places to Stay in Asia'. It was also one of two hotels in mainland China to be ranked by *Institutional Investor* among the 'Top 100 Hotels in the World' in 2007. Offering distinguished service, St Regis remains one of the city's top luxury destinations for travellers who wish to experience a more traditional side of the Orient.

About half of St Regis' 273 guestrooms are suites which offer decadent living quarters furnished with inviting sofas, deluxe beds and exquisite, antique Chinese furniture. Every room is fitted with a DVD player, high-speed Internet access, and a personal fax line. Visitors are pampered by St Regis' trademark butler service that provides round-the-clock services including the unpacking and packing of luggage, shoe shining, and complimentary tea and coffee. Visitors can also send their wishes to butlers via email and receive confirmation via return email for requests such as dinner reservations and booking of theatre tickets.

As the first luxury city spa with natural hot-spring jacuzzis in Beijing, St Regis Spa and Club provides travellers with the extravagances of late-night pampering. It incorporates a thermal jacuzzi, whirlpool, aromatic steam room with saunas and cool plunge pools. Surrounded by glass walls, the 25-m (82-ft) indoor pool is flooded with sunlight by day, and at night, it offers spectacular garden views.

The hotel's signature restaurant, Danieli's, has garnered numerous accolades for its rustic, regional cuisine while Astor Grill is the epitome of fine dining, renowned for its steaks and seafood grill. Richly decorated with Chinese screens and delicate pottery, Celestial Court is a picture of Asian opulence, enabling diners to enjoy authentic cuisine from southern China in style. For relaxing after-dinner drinks, travellers can head for the Press Club Bar which will take them back in time to the heyday of the Beijing International Club with its live jazz and cigars.

ROOMS
273

FOOD
Astor Grill: steakhouse and seafood •
Celestial Court: Cantonese • Danieli's:
Italian • Shunsai: Japanese •
The Garden Court: international

DRINK
Press Club Bar • Garden Lounge •
Cigar Lounge • Wine Lounge

FEATURES
St Regis Spa and Club •
Roman-style indoor pool •
squash court • golf driving area •
bowling alley • 24-hour butler service

NEARBY
Ancient Observatory • Silk Street
Market • Ritan Park • Wangfujing
Avenue • Forbidden City

CONTACT
21 Jianguomenwai Avenue
Chaoyang District, Beijing 100020 •
telephone: +86.10.6460 6688 •
facsimile: +86.10.6460 3299 •
email: stregis.beijing@stregis.com •
website: www.stregis.com/beijing

st regis spa + club

...the first luxury city spa with natural hot-spring jacuzzis in Beijing.

Strategically located in St Regis Hotel, Beijing, St Regis Spa and Club can be accessed by its main entrance on Xiushui North Street or by the south corridor that connects to the hotel. Its well-placed locale, neighbouring the famed Beijing International Club, is attractive to business and leisure travellers to Beijing.

Covering an area of 1,500 sq m (16,146 sq ft), St Regis Spa and Club is the first luxury city spa with natural hot-spring jacuzzis in Beijing. Travellers can chill out in relaxation lounges with personal headsets. A 25-m (82-ft) Roman-style indoor pool is encased by glass walls while the bar which overlooks the pool provides swimmers with rest areas and refreshments. By night, bathers can enjoy spectacular garden views—an inspiring distraction from swimming lengths. After their workouts, they can make use of the thermal whirlpools, saunas, jacuzzis, and cool plunge pools.

Using Jurlique products, treatments at St Regis Spa and Club incorporate aromatherapy, herbal medicine, homeopathy, botanical and marine sciences to provide therapies that are organic and pH-balanced. Physicians skilled in traditional Chinese medicine and massage are on hand to provide a variety of treatments such as Beijing Body Renewal which lasts two and a half hours. It consists of a full-body hot-oil wrap with relaxing acupressure massage on the scalp, followed by an extensive hydrating and fully restorative treatment for both the hands and feet.

Visitors can choose from aromatic baths, deluxe body wraps, reflexology and toning treatments such as a 30-minute Re-energising Express Travel Massage, designed to revitalise the body and restore regular sleep patterns.

Influenced by the philosophies of Chinese massage, St Regis Spa Signature Treatment and Spa Cuisine incorporates a full-body deep-tissue aromatherapy massage to release naturally calming endorphins. It is then followed by a

THIS PAGE: Visitors can cool off in the palatial indoor pool.
OPPOSITE (FROM TOP): Over 40 Eastern and Western massage styles and treatments are available at the spa; the fitness centre is fitted with strength-training equipment, cardio machines and 35 TV sets; the relaxing ambience prepares travellers for spa sessions.

ROOMS
10 treatment rooms

FEATURES
aromatherapy steam rooms •
natural hot-spring spa •
Roman-style indoor pool •
squash court • golf driving area •
bowling alley • 24-hour butler service

NEARBY
Ancient Observatory • Silk Street
Market • Ritan Park • Wangfujing
Avenue • Forbidden City

CONTACT
St Regis Hotel, Beijing
21 Jianguomenwai Avenue
Chaoyang District, Beijing 100020 •
telephone: +86.10.6460 6688 •
facsimile: +86.10.6460 3299 •
email: stregis.beijing@stregis.com •
website: www.stregis.com/beijing

rejuvenating facial using personalised nutrients and antioxidants. Whilst still in a state of relaxation, visitors can then enjoy a two-course meal prepared by the hotel's chef to optimise health and wellness. For the ultimate indulgence, the spa offers VIP treatment suites that include a hot mineral-spring bath, aromatherapy steam rooms and a tekevision set.

St Regis Spa and Club is a membership-based spa and leisure club while hotel and apartment residents enjoy complimentary usage of the spa and club. Alongside thermal bliss and sybaritic pampering, travellers have access to a fitness centre which is open 24 hours a day, two squash courts, billiards and snooker rooms, an eight-lane bowling centre, golf driving area and putting green. Visitors can also choose from fitness classes such as pilates, taichi, yoga, spinning, and ballet for children.

zenspa

...allows one to enter into such a deep state of relaxation...

Located in a traditional Chinese courtyard house, Zenspa provides a tranquil and luxurious retreat in the midst of China's bustling capital. Offering full-day treatments, visitors can relax in the open courtyard, indulge in the private treatment suites and admire the intricate architecture of this beautiful, centuries-old building.

Whilst the exterior retains all the original features such as curved tiled roofs, intricate motifs, beautifully restored lattice screens and wooden columns in brilliant red, the interior follows a striking, minimalist style. The design, created by acclaimed Hong Kong-based David Ng from Match It, incorporates elements of antique furniture, stones and wooden planks to create a modern, yet natural atmosphere. His signature lacquer boxes in startlingly vivid colours complement the rustic tones of the surrounding bare wood. With a contemporary tension pool, precise stone cladding and customised furniture, the overall visual effect is simply stunning.

Adopting a holistic approach to the physical and spiritual well-being of its clients, Zenspa provides a sanctuary for visitors. It introduces new spa therapies on a regular basis and offers one of the widest selection of treatments in the city.

Travellers can choose from therapeutic sessions that hail from Eastern and Western philosophies. The treatments include naturopathy, clinical aromatherapy and Ayurvedic Shirodhara therapies, as well as Thai and Indonesian herbal massages. Two saunas and a relaxation area are also available for visitors to unwind in.

A popular treatment is Ultimate Indulgence which lasts four and a half hours. It consists of a body scrub using gold leaves, imported Thai herbs and rose petals, followed by a pure honey wrap and a choice of Royal Thai Floral Bath or Cleopatra Milk Bath. The finishing touch is the spa's signature Burmese Thanaka facial.

Cleopatra Milk Bath was introduced as Egyptian queen Cleopatra's legendary beauty was attributed to a daily bath in fresh milk. Scientists have also discovered that lactic acid which is found in fresh milk naturally dissolves the 'glue' that holds dead skin cells to the body. Roses contain therapeutic natural oils which have a softening effect on the skin, while many Chinese believe that gold leaves give a boost to one's internal energy, also known as 'chi'.

THIS PAGE (FROM TOP): *Ground Chinese herbs are used in therapeutic treatments; the Chinese courtyard house is a picture of serenity.*

OPPOSITE (CLOCKWISE FROM TOP LEFT): *Hot herbal compresses are applied in massages to soothe warm oil over the body; ear candling has a calming effect and can lull one to sleep; a time for quiet contemplation.*

At Zenspa, visitors can expect to be pampered with a wide range of services that include body scrubs, body wraps, massages and facial care.

Other luxurious body wraps include the Detox Seaweed Body Masque, Rejuvenating Thai Herbal Body Masque, Moisturising Honey Body Masque, Deep-Cleansing Yoghurt Body Masque and the Green Tea Body Masque, an antioxidant-rich blend meant to boost the body's immune system, enhance the metabolism and eliminate toxins. The healing effect of Japanese green tea also protects the skin from stress and pollution, leaving the complexion fresher, healthier and better oxygenated.

One of the more popular treatments is the Rejuventating Thai Herbal Body masque which replenishes the skin with essential vitamins. This traditional therapy uses natural ingredients such as green oranges, prai roots, mint, cucumbers and honey.

THIS PAGE (FROM TOP): In the relaxation room, guests can wind down after an invigorating massage; visitors can enjoy snacks at the lounge area.

OPPOSITE: Zenspa is a sanctuary for visitors to retreat to in the midst of the hustle and bustle of downtown Beijing.

ROOMS
reflexology treatment room • 4 VIP suites • 5 private rooms

FEATURES
treatments • massages • snack bar • facials • reflexology • Vichy shower • lounge

NEARBY
Beijing Amusement Park • Temple of Heaven Park • Ancient Observatory

CONTACT
House 1, 8A Xiaowuji Road Chaoyang District, Beijing 100023 • telephone: +86.10.8731 2530 • facsimile: +86.10.8731 2539 • email: info@zenspa.com.cn • website: www.zenspa.com.cn

To combat Beijing's bitter winter months, Zenspa has formulated a bath comprising rock sugar and ginger. Designed to nourish dry skin and improve blood circulation, it is based on an ancient remedy from southern China. The spa therapists are also skilled in a variety of massages. Visitors can try a traditional Thai massage whereby the masseur uses the elbows, forearms, knees and feet to apply pressure, creating a smooth energy flow within the body to help loosen joints and stretch muscles.

One of the most luxurious treatments offered at Zenspa is the four-handed massage that has been likened to a choreographed dance with masseurs working in perfect co-ordination to eliminate stress and tension. Visitors can also try the Vichy shower therapy which includes a

scrub. Moisturising, rejuvenating, whitening and deep-cleansing facial treatments add a glow to the body.

Visitors are encouraged to enjoy Zenspa's soothing ambience after the completion of their treatments so as to maintain their peaceful state of mind. A lounge area and a bar which serves healthy snacks and juices provide ideal surroundings for relaxation.

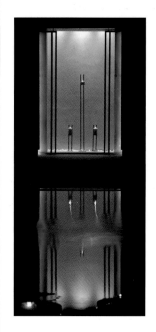

danieli's

...the feeling of being transported to the rolling hills and olive rows of Tuscany.

THIS PAGE: *St Regis' signature restaurant is overwhelmingly popular with discerning diners.*

OPPOSITE (CLOCKWISE FROM TOP): *Diners can look forward to impeccable service at Danieli's; a tantalising variety of northern and central Italian cuisine; the classical Italian ambience is accentuated by the hand-painted ceiling details, antique ornaments and candelabra.*

Located on the second floor of St Regis Hotel, Danieli's is considered by many to be far and away the best Italian restaurant in town. Known and acclaimed for its traditional and impeccable service, the hotel's signature restaurant is always bustling with local Chinese, expatriates, and hotel visitors luxuriating within its rustic elegance.

Stepping through the arched entrance into Danieli's, visitors get the feeling of being transported to the rolling hills and olive rows of Tuscany. The hand-painted ceiling, stone columns, terracotta-tiled floor, and rich yellow tones evoke a hearty warmth juxtaposed only by the urban landscape of Beijing seen through the green shuttered windows. Large potted plants, hanging candelabra and whimsical paintings further contribute to the homely scene.

While chefs toss fresh pasta and flame succulent meats in the kitchen, the service staff attend to diners unobtrusively to ensure a perfect dining experience. Over lunch, light pastas and delicious antipasto attract a diverse set looking for a lively atmosphere while in the evening, the restaurant is the epitome of understated elegance.

Focusing on northern and central Italian cuisine, chef Marco Mazzei presents a tantalising menu of seasonal specialities. Using traditional methods, he keeps the food simple, yet full of flavour. This approach has undoubtedly enabled Danieli's to clinch the award for 'Beijing's Best Italian Restaurant' from the Beijing Tourism Administration, among numerous accolades from local publications.

Diners can choose from a fascinating spread of appetisers of grilled vegetables, seafood, mozzarella and carpaccio. Favourites include Parma Ham with Marinated Artichoke Hearts, Tomato and Artichoke Risotto with Truffle Oil, Mushroom Salad flavoured with Lemon Oil, and Smoked Duck Breast with Duck Liver, Scallop, and Shrimp. Pasta lovers will have a field day with the extensive list of pasta dishes which range from the light and tangy Penne Pasta tossed with Scallops, Bacon, Garlic and Zucchini to heavier, gamey treats such as Pasta laced with Pheasant and Truffles.

At Danieli's, main courses are served in large, hearty portions. With a veritable spread of seafood and tender steaks, diners are spoilt for choice. To end the meal on a sweet note, they can sample desserts such as Marinated Prunes Ice Parfait on Pistachio Sauce, Amaretto-flavoured Sabayon with Vanilla Ice Cream, and Parmesan Cheese with Fresh Pears. The restaurant also has an extensive selection of the finest Italian wines to accompany the traditional regional cuisine, setting visitors up for an unforgettable experience at Danieli's.

SEATS
68

FOOD
northern and central Italian

DRINK
extensive wine list

FEATURES
authentic Italian atmosphere •
fine dining

NEARBY
Ancient Observatory • Silk Street
Market • Ritan Park • Wangfujing
Avenue • Forbidden City

CONTACT
St Regis Hotel, Beijing
21 Jianguomenwai Avenue
Chaoyang District, Beijing 100020 •
telephone: +86.10.6460 6688
ext 2441 •
facsimile: +86.10.6460 3299 •
email: stregis.beijing@stregis.com •
website: www.stregis.com/beijing

face

...heavy beams and huge antique wooden doors evoke a rustic warmth.

Tucked away in a lane near the south entrance of Workers' Stadium, Face offers visitors respite from Beijing's bustling streets. Comprising Face Bar and two restaurants—Lan Na Thai and Hazara—Face is a lifestyle and food and beverage complex spread across two floors of a refurbished space that was formerly a school. Each room is painted in a range of vibrant colours, from midnight blue to opulent red. Wooden floorboards, heavy beams and huge antique wooden doors evoke a rustic warmth. The artefacts and furniture in the bar and restaurants were sourced from Indonesia, Thailand, India and China.

The Thai restaurant, Lan Na Thai, is named after an ancient kingdom in northern Thailand. Its name translates to 'land of a million rice fields'. The restaurant features white swathes of muslin softly draping the intricately carved dark wooden beams and columns, creating a romantic ambience.

Popular appetisers include the Gai Hor Bai Toey Pandan Chicken, a tempting dish of succulent fried chicken pieces wrapped in fragrant pandan leaf, Crisp Spring Rolls, and Tod Man Pla which are deep-fried fish cakes served with a spicy sauce.

THIS PAGE (CLOCKWISE FROM ABOVE): Face complex is located in a renovated 1970s schoolhouse; Lan Na Thai is lavishly furnished with paintings and sculptures; Hazara has a wide variety of tempting north Indian dishes.

OPPOSITE (CLOCKWISE FROM TOP): The tranquil ambience of Face Bar; delectable samosas at Hazara; Face Bar's design incorporates an eclectic mix of design styles.

Diners can also sample the aromatic soups made from ingredients such as lemongrass chicken and coconut prawns. Tasty stir-fries, piquant curries, charcoal grills and oven-cooked dishes are all delicately flavoured with Thai spices and herbs.

Hazara, the namesake of a tribe and region in Afghanistan, specialises in wok and tandoor cooking, which is a blend of healthy country and royal cuisines associated with northern India. Dishes include Murgh Makhni (butter chicken), Gosht Khorma (cashew nut lamb curry) and Tawa Machli (fish seasoned with chilli coriander). Diners at Hazara can choose from more than 10 types of Indian bread, from a simple naan to a pudina parontha, a layered wholewheat bread with chopped mint leaves.

Diners can then go to Face Bar for a relaxing post-prandial drink. One can recline on the Chinese daybeds, luxuriating in the stylish surrounds; the less sedentarily inclined may play a game of pool. Visitors can also sit back in the deep wicker chairs, spread out along the terrace overlooking a long arboreal lawn including a row of six magnificent mature poplars.

SEATS
Face: 120 indoor, 70 outdoor • Lan Na Thai: 70 • Hazara: 88

FOOD
Lan Na Thai: classical Thai • Hazara: north Indian

DRINK
Face

FEATURES
garden • pool table • private dining rooms• Chinese daybeds • terrace

NEARBY
Workers' Stadium • Sanlitun • Ritan Park • Dongyue Temple

CONTACT
26 East Caoyuan, South Gongti Road Chaoyang District, Beijing 100020 • telephone: +86.10.6551 6788 • facsimile: +86.10.6551 6739 • email: beijing@facebars.com • website: www.facebars.com

green t. house

GREEN T. HOUSE, a combination of teahouse and restaurant with art exhibitions and cultural events, is the vision of musician, designer and tea master JinR. GREEN T. HOUSE started in 1997 as an intimate teahouse, inspired by JinR's growing collection of china that could no longer fit into her apartment. Over the years it has built itself a remarkable international reputation for its blend of innovative design and New China cuisine, and has become one of the hottest destinations in Beijing for locals and visitors alike.

The concept is a surprising blend of sophistication and whimsy. A stark white backdrop sets a minimalist tone softened by billowing sheets of muslin and low hanging white Chinese lanterns. The central focus rests on a long table, stretching the length of the restaurant, set with high-backed chairs that tower well over guests' heads. Abstract pieces of furniture that are changed every so often are positioned across the room, provoking conversation and commentary, and guests are often delighted by the newest additions. A long, smooth white bar and similarly pristine bar stools seem to float in the distance, an illusion wrought by the dramatically bleached background. The effect is stunning—an authentically Chinese atmosphere with interior design that might be found in a glossy magazine. Promoting local art and featuring ad hoc cultural performances, guests are continually delighted by the extraordinary and energetic atmosphere here.

The culinary experience at GREEN T. HOUSE is as stimulating as its setting. Specialising in New China cuisine, traditional techniques are melded with surprising twists, familiar ingredients and spices combined in unexpected ways. The menu is designed to tantalise and challenge, and the tea-infused recipes certainly do all of this and more. The presentation is impeccable—rose petals, bamboo and other natural materials are used to create artwork out of every dish.

THIS PAGE (CLOCKWISE FROM BOTTOM):
The unusual pieces of furniture are striking conversation starters; sheer white lengths of fabric and translucent hand-painted lanterns create a light, modernistic feel; New China cuisine is on the menu at GREEN T. HOUSE.

OPPOSITE (FROM TOP): GREEN T. HOUSE is furnished with a fine sense of fun and playful design; each dish is presented with style and flair, using natural elements; the eye is immediately drawn to the centrepiece table and chairs.

The selection of hand-blended teas is an integral part of the GREEN T. HOUSE experience. Focusing on the long history of tea-drinking in China, GREEN T. HOUSE sets to re-establish this time-honoured ritual with China's younger and hipper generation. Using family-style open seating, they encourage guests to relax, build friendships and converse as would occur in a more traditional teahouse environment in the olden days.

· GREEN T. HOUSE has artfully created a sophisticated, modern spin on a number of very important and age-old Chinese values that have been deeply integral to this rich culture over the centuries. Attracting an eclectic crowd, the stylish premises are filled with a warm, lively atmosphere as guests and visitors come from all over to experience the new China.

SEATS
150

FOOD
New China

DRINK
extensive wine list • cocktails • tea

FEATURES
modern design • art displays • cultural performances

NEARBY
Workers' Stadium • Sanlitun

CONTACT
6 West Gongti Road
Chaoyang District, Beijing 100027 •
telephone: +86.10.6552 8310/11 •
facsimile: +86.10.6553 8750 •
email: reservations@green-t-house.com •
website: www.green-t-house.com

green t. house living

...a luxurious escape from the city.

In 1997, musician and designer JinR redefined luxury dining in Beijing with the opening of GREEN T. HOUSE, a combination of teahouse and restaurant, whose remarkable design continues to receive worldwide publicity and high-profile patronage today. Starting as an intimate teahouse, the brand has now diversified into a lifestyle concept, with the sponsorship and hosting of cultural events and art exhibitions, and a luxurious escape from the city.

Located near the Wen Yu River, a short 20 minutes' drive towards the airport from Beijing's bustling centre, GREEN T. HOUSE Living is set in a vast 15,000-sq-m (161,500-sq-ft) complex. Conceived, designed and decorated entirely by owner JinR, the bold Zhanguo period-inspired building rises from a wide expanse of spacious, terraced courtyards. Built from white stone, the sleek lines and symmetrical walls provide visitors with a welcome taste of pure architectural Zen. Inside, the minimalist style continues, creating a refreshingly calm space flooded with natural light. A large white chimney floats over an elongated fireplace and giant, patterned Chinese lanterns hang from the arched roof. A polished white stone floor set with smooth crystal

THIS PAGE: The magnificently wide and spacious GREEN T. HOUSE Living, flooded with natural light.

OPPOSITE (CLOCKWISE FROM BOTTOM): The Orientalist screens provide brief glimpses of the activities within; low tables for an afternoon of communal tea-drinking and chat; all the teas at GREEN T. HOUSE Living are processed by hand.

is interrupted at intervals by central communal tables. Traditional low tables and Chinese chairs are meticulously set up for tea ceremonies, where guests can enjoy views of the surrounding countryside through the full-height glass windows on every side.

The cuisine at GREEN T. HOUSE Living befits the elegant and natural surroundings, with tea-based dishes that blend fresh, natural ingredients with time-honoured, traditional cooking techniques from across regions of China. Dishes, however, are far from rustic, and include delectable creations such as the delicate Scallop Blossoms in Snow, the popular Green Tea Dumplings and the succulent Tender Oriental Touch on Beef Tenderloin. Tea plays an important, even pivotal, role in the GREEN T. HOUSE experience and their many home-made blends can be leisurely enjoyed during afternoon tea or along with a full tea ceremony and tea snacks.

Whilst guests visit primarily to enjoy the unique New China cuisine and take in the startling design, GREEN T. HOUSE Living also offers further enticements for visitors to make the short journey to the outskirts of Beijing. The Tearoom, an arrestingly bold and modern glass interpretation of the traditional teahouse, with a range of hand-blended teas and herbal and medicinal tea offerings; the Bath, a striking and starkly tranquil space offering contemporary renderings of ancient and traditional Chinese therapies and healing philosophies; and the Retreat, an ultra-luxurious open-plan lodging villa with sweeping, panoramic views of the surrounding countryside and open-air jacuzzi and fireplace.

SEATS
50+

FOOD
New China

DRINK
teahouse • extensive wine list

FEATURES
modern design • tranquil space • courtyard • art displays • music and cultural performances

NEARBY
The Orchard • 798 Dashanzi Art District • Airport

CONTACT
318 Hegezhuang Village Cuigezhuang Township Chaoyang District, Beijing 100015 • telephone: +86.10.6434 2519 or +86.10.8456 6422 • email: reservations@green-t-house.com • website: www.green-t-house.com

hatsune

...a favourite with all who venture through its doors.

THIS PAGE (FROM LEFT): Expert chefs prepare contemporary Japanese dishes using fresh ingredients; each dish is artfully presented; the rolls are a favourite with all.

OPPOSITE (CLOCKWISE FROM TOP LEFT): Sunken tables provide comfort with a touch of authenticity; expect a warm welcome from the friendly and helpful staff; a tempting display of sushi; one can expect great food in stylish settings at Hatsune.

Having been honoured with accolades from publications from across the globe, including frequent awards from local expatriate magazines, Hatsune—often alongside sister restaurant Kagen—is commonly referred to as the best Japanese restaurant in town. Combining service, style and outstanding sushi to create its refreshing and playful atmosphere, Hatsune has become a favourite with all who venture through its doors. The passions of Hatsune's owner, Alan Wong, are built into the menu and design of the restaurant, and his devotion to dining has rubbed off on the rest of the staff who provide a level of service rarely seen in China.

Designed by Alan Wong himself, the interior is fun and completely contemporary, yet still manages to exude the more traditional, zen-like qualities of an authentic Japanese eatery. A sleek glass and metal entrance is softened by a loose carpet of smooth pebbles scattered across the floor. Bamboo pathways lead around the minimalist dining area to the bathrooms and main entrance. Tatami tables are dramatically underlit by stylised lamps. At one end of the restaurant, a long, wide sushi bar attracts constant attention and guests can watch the blurred hands of masterful chefs as they race across chopping boards with their practised knifework. Throughout the restaurant, unconventional details add a sense of quirkiness and give Hatsune its unique style.

Catering for short business lunches, long romantic dinners and large celebrations, the restaurant bustles through the day with a constant stream of chattering locals and gregarious expats.

With seemingly limitless energy, Hatsune dedicates huge enthusiasm and skill to its enticing and innovative menu. Bento boxes are filled with exciting and unusual treats ideal for a quick lunch. One can also sample the varied menu which also features an impressive selection of sashimi, tempura, teriyaki, sushi, yakitori, grilled fish, rice and noodle dishes. Using only the freshest produce means that all the flavours that emerge from the kitchen are bursting with subtle nuance. Hatsune's rolls have become famous throughout the city for their inventive combinations. Favourites include the Beijing roll with Roast Duck, 119 roll filled with Tuna and a Tangy Sauce and the California Roll stuffed with Crab and Avocado.

With a growing network that includes Kagen, Haiku by Hatsune in Shanghai, and a third restaurant in Beijing scheduled to open later this year, Alan Wong has created in Hatsune a high-energy rollercoaster ride for the taste buds and an atmosphere that will appeal to all—be sure to make a reservation, as its popularity will only rise in the days ahead.

SEATS
130

FOOD
contemporary Japanese

DRINK
extensive wine and sake list

FEATURES
sushi bar • tatami seating

NEARBY
China World Hotel • Ritan Park

CONTACT:
Heqiao Group Building C #201
8A Guanghua Road
Chaoyang District, Beijing 100026 •
telephone: +86.10.6581 3939 •
facsimile: +86.10.6583 2133 •
email: hatsunesushi@yahoo.com

house by the park

...sophisticated and intimate surroundings...

THIS PAGE: House By The Park is known for its creative, stylish design, drawing the hip and fashionable crowds to its doors.

OPPOSITE (CLOCKWISE FROM TOP): Lamb Shank with Garlic Foam, served up with flair in a martini glass; the simple elegance of the clear glass tableware underscores the menu of innovative haute cuisine; food presentation is impeccable.

Established in February 2006, House By The Park is Singapore-based Tung Lok Group's second restaurant in Beijing. The Group is responsible for more than 20 restaurants in Asia, including My Humble House located in Singapore, Beijing, Tokyo and New Delhi, The Chinoise Story in Shanghai and Wuhan, and Taipan in Jakarta and Medan.

The interior design firm behind House By The Park's décor has made liberal use of a selection of dark woods, slate flooring and atmospheric, sombre colours to evoke a quiet sophistication and intimacy that subtly infuses the surroundings. At one end, chrome stools and deep leather sofas provide a comfortable setting for pre- or post-dinner drinks at the bar.

Discreet booths enable the diners to have more privacy behind elegant screens of bright chrome while vast windows overlook the lush greenery of a small park below, creating a bright contrast to the dark, urban interior.

Innovative lighting systems are used to their full advantage throughout this space. Lamps by German designers Ingo Maurer and Swiss-based Belux are carefully placed in a zigzag pattern on the ceiling and on low tables, adding to the sense of stylish intimacy. Other lamps of the distinctive Maurer design—Zettel, Birdie and Jimken—can also be seen about the restaurant.

The chefs combine ingredients from around the world with traditional and modern Chinese cooking methods to create a mouth-watering and varied menu. Unusual appetisers feature Tuna Tartar with Mango Salsa in a Popiah Cone and Lime Sherbet in Lemongrass Jelly.

Other delicacies include Braised Shark's Fin with Flower Crabmeat served with a Hot and Sour Consommé; the labour-intensive Six-Hour Braised Pork Trotters with Lotus Seeds and Edamame Beans in a Red Wine Sauce; Pan-fried Freshwater King Prawns with a Lemon Infused

Spicy Sauce; and the popular Bamboo and Wine-marinated Chicken with Honshimeiji and Asparagus.

House By The Park is located in China Central Place, one of Beijing's newest developments in Xicheng which is an increasingly vibrant commercial district on the west side of Houhai Lake. The large complex is also home to offices, residential towers and the Ritz-Carlton Beijing, Central Place.

SEATS
150

FOOD
modern Chinese

DRINK
extensive wine list • cocktails

FEATURES
bar • semi-private dining rooms

NEARBY
China Central Place • Xicheng • Houhai Lake

CONTACT
2/F Club House, Block 19
China Central Place, 89 Jianguo Road
Chaoyang District, Beijing 100025 •
telephone: +86.10.6530 7770 •
facsimile: +86.10.6530 7771 •
email: housebythepark@tunglok.com •
website: tunglok.com/housebythepark

kagen

...a stylish underground retreat.

Specialising in teppanyaki, Japanese hot pot and barbecue cuisine, Kagen is a stylish underground retreat. Tucked beneath its sister restaurant Hatsune, it shares the quirky inventive design, the delicious cuisine and lively atmosphere that has made the group so popular and steadfast in a city where restaurant signs and addresses change weekly.

Kagen's sense of humour is first felt at the doorway. With no doorbell or doorknob, newcomers often find themselves a little confused. Those in the know, however, simply swipe their hand under the red light and the heavyset door automatically opens, revealing the way down a curving pathway toward the visually stunning interior. Using hardy industrial materials including concrete, stainless steel and granite, the design is sharp and minimalist. Softened by the intimate lighting, luxurious seats and copper bar, Kagen retains an air of warmth and comfort. Raked sand pathways and stylish water features evoke the calm of a Japanese garden whilst the vibe remains firmly set in urban chic.

THIS PAGE (CLOCKWISE FROM TOP): The underfloor lighting gives a soft, warm glow to Kagen's interiors; the unique restaurant entrance; water features evoke the feel of a tranquil Japanese garden.

OPPOSITE (FROM TOP): The bustling restaurant is the ideal place for a sociable dinner with friends; enjoy a well-made cocktail from the extensive list of beverages.

SEATS
175

FOOD
shabu shabu • yaki niku • teppanyaki

DRINK
extensive wine and sake list • cocktails

FEATURES
lounge area • cooking at the table

NEARBY
China World Hotel • Ritan Park

CONTACT
Heqiao Group Building B1
8A Guanghua Road
Chaoyang District, Beijing 100026 •
telephone: +86.10.6581 3939 •
facsimile: +86.10.6583 2133 •
email: hatsunesushi@yahoo.com

Kagen means 'the origin of fire', providing the basic concept of its delicious menu. Hot pot, known as shabu shabu, and barbecue dishes, known as yaki niku, are cooked at the table. It's a fun and relaxed way to enjoy a sociable meal, while the teppanyaki section provides an ideal opportunity to witness the skilled chefs at work. Using high-end cuts of raw meats and fresh vegetables, the cuisine on offer is simple, hearty and surprisingly flavourful. Kagen offers several soup broths, including miso with black shoots, seafood and sukiyaki, in which to cook the meat, adding subtle nuances to the flavours. Premium cuts include marbled Kobe beef, rib-eye, fatty pork, lean pork and chicken. Kagen also caters to vegetarians with a delicious variety of greens to cook in the broth. For barbecuing, guests can choose from a wide selection, including Beijing roast duck, pork spare ribs, sirloin steak, yakitori chicken skewers, prawns and squid. Teppanyaki is served from an equally extensive menu of options.

After dinner, guests can continue the night's revelries in the open lounge area. Comfortable seats surround the industrial-style concrete bar, a lively gathering place at the end of the evening. An extensive wine and sake list, several dozen martinis and some rather large and innovative cocktails, most notably the 'yukiko', which uses shiso leaves instead of mint in a Japanese twist on the mojito, are certain to keep satisfied spirits high.

the dining room

...spectacular views of the lush golf course.

THIS PAGE (FROM RIGHT): *The Dining Room counts diplomats among its guests; natural lighting is used to great effect at the restaurant.*

OPPOSITE (CLOCKWISE FROM TOP): *Clean lines dominate in one of the private dining areas; dining with a difference; delectable Chinese fare; diners can admire the artefacts which adorn the walls.*

The Dining Room, which forms part of the Clubhouse at Bayhood No. 9, is set amidst undulating hills, pine forests, lakes and waterfalls. Covering 133 hectares (329 acres), Bayhood No. 9 is an exclusive premier golf club and resort, designed by award-winning Canadian firm Nelson and Haworth Golf Course Architects.

The restaurant, The Dining Room, is open to both members and non-members alike. It is made up of 18 private dining areas, including four separate villas which afford spectacular views of the lush golf course. The décor of each dining room reflects the different styles of dynasties in China's history through the clever use of accessories such as silk embroidery, chinaware, pottery, Beijing opera stage props, Chinese seals and origami.

The gourmet kitchen is headed by chef Xi Guolong who, for many years, has entertained world leaders with his innovative Chinese cuisine. Throughout his career, he has prepared meals for former Chinese president Jiang Zemin, former British prime minister Tony Blair and Vladimir Putin, the president of the Russian Federation.

Guests at The Dining Room can sample Chinese Royal Emperor's Dim Sum, said to be a favourite of former Chinese premier Zhou Enlai. Other dishes offered at the restaurant include Sichuan Chicken and Bacon Strips in Tibetan Saffron, and Fresh Scallop, Sea Cucumber and Fish Maw in Superior Chicken Broth.

Besides The Dining Room, visitors can also make use of the massage facilities at the Clubhouse which overlooks a large natural lake at the 18th hole. A towering atrium which reaches to three storeys is flooded in light streaming down from the glass roof. Large pillars are bolstered with old wooden beams while church candles line the aisle to the reception area.

Visitors can also make trips to the majestic Summer Palace, the Great Wall, the ancient Ming Tombs and the Temple of the Heavenly Mother, a 300-year-old Taoist temple which has been restored to its former glory by Bayhood No. 9.

SEATS
270

FOOD
Cantonese fusion

DRINK
bar • members' lounge

FEATURES
18 private dining rooms

NEARBY
Summer Palace • Great Wall (Badaling section) • Ming Tombs

CONTACT
Bayhood No. 9
9 Anwai Beihu
Chaoyang District, Beijing 100012 •
telephone: +86.10.8491 9797 •
facsimile: 86.10.6491 8888 •
email: info@bayhood9.com •
website: www.bayhood9.com

the orchard

...an idyllic setting for organic lunches and dinners.

THIS PAGE (FROM TOP): *The restaurant offers a fine menu of Continental European cuisine, created with organic home-grown ingredients; locally produced scarves hand-knit by women from the nearby village are available in the shop.*

OPPOSITE (CLOCKWISE FROM TOP): *Green plants frame the shop entrance; a quirky sense of décor suffuses the compound, juxtaposing dark wood chairs with bright settees; the picturesque garden paths cut through the landscaped grounds; warm colours set visitors at ease.*

The Orchard is a rustic haven accessed via a long driveway through rows of apple trees. Only 20 minutes by taxi from the city centre, The Orchard is an idyllic setting for organic lunches and dinners.

Owners Lisa Minder Wu and Wu 'Ertao' Yun Tao took over the land when it was no more than a few trees and a pond. They have lovingly created a refuge that now features a beautiful restaurant, stylish coffee shop, retail boutique shop, three organic greenhouses, a teahouse and lake.

Caring for more than 1,000 apple, pear, peach, persimmon and pomegranate trees as well as growing its own herbs and vegetables, The Orchard is known for its organically home-grown produce. They specialise in Western cuisine and appetisers include Sorrel and Potato Soup; and Winter Vegetable Ratatouille with Stuffed

Roasted Tomato, Soft Polenta and Parmesan. Tasty salads are drizzled in vinaigrettes filled with home-grown herbs and include an Arugula Salad with Strawberries, Pine Nuts and Aged Tibetan Yak Cheese; Roasted Duck Breast and Beet Salad with Fennel-Orange Dressing. Mains include Ribeye Steak with Truffle Butter, Potato-Cauliflower Gratin and Spinach; and Succulent Chicken.

The boutique shop at The Orchard sells various furniture and home products. With their own craftsmen located on-site, the owners design whimsical pieces of furniture and accessories using wood, iron, copper, silver, glass, leather and fabric. Guests can also buy sauces and pickles made by the chef. The shop also represents various designers such as Nicolas Favard who crafts modern silver and gold jewellery, Gabrielle Harris who designs ancient motif silver jewellery under her own label

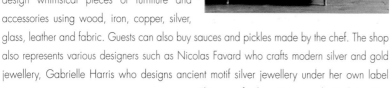

Things of the Jing; and Kathrin Von Rechenberg who creates rare tea silk clothing. The shop also sells beaded bags and animal figures made by handicapped orphans from Hebei province and other products to benefit local hospitals and orphaned infants.

The proud owners of The Orchard have succeeded in creating a community spirit through their active involvement in the local neighbourhood. They have also set up a school which opens during weekends for the village children, re-built a bridge and employed local women to hand-knit scarves and other products for sale in their retail section.

FOOD
Continental European

DRINK
teahouse • café

SHOP
clothes • jewellery • furniture

FEATURES
orchard • lake • boutique • home-grown organic ingredients

NEARBY
798 Dashanzi Art District • airport

CONTACT
Hegezhuang Village
Cuigezhuang Township
Chaoyang District, Beijing 100103 •
telephone: +86.139.1121 1965 •
email: theorchardbj@yahoo.com

centro bar + lounge

...Centro exudes sultry sophistication in a palette of claret and gold.

Shangri-La's Kerry Centre Hotel, Beijing has already made its mark as the centre of activity for the city's well-heeled elite, who gather each night at the hotel's stylish bar and lounge, Centro. Designed by Darryl W Goveas of Pure Creative Asia, who has worked his brand of magic on plush spots such as various Christian Dior boutiques around Asia and Hong Kong's Alibi Restaurant and Bar, Centro exudes sultry sophistication in a palette of claret and gold.

The bar is an arresting showpiece in itself, with inset lights that impart a soft luminescence to the surrounding environment and backed by a textured wall feature of glass on wood with a metallic, hammered finish. Alternatively, guests can head to an elevated platform, where lush, inviting sofas beckon. By day, sunlight streams through the room, bestowing it with a fresh, natural glow. By night, ambient light from scattered coloured lamps exudes sensuality.

Like any self-respecting über bar, Centro boasts a wine cellar that stores up to 500 bottles. So far, more than 30 varieties of wine are served by the glass in oversized Reidel glasses, while chilled bottles are presented in unique cone-shaped wine buckets designed by Philippe Starck. To take the guesswork out of choosing wines, Centro's wine list comes with a twist—rather than standard paper or cardboard menus, it is presented on wireless PC tablets that are linked to the websites of major international vineyards.

Apart from the vast selection of fine vintages, guests can choose from an extensive list of cocktails from martinis to mojitos. In the meantime, sway to the live music of some of the world's best bands. Besides its undeniably chic décor and impressive drinks list, one of Centro's key strengths, and a strong draw for those with a discerning ear, is its commitment to bringing in the best musical talents from around the world.

On busy nights, guests can also book the bar's private room that seats up to 10 people comfortably (standing room only will fit up to 25). The best part is that Centro is open 24 hours a day, which means Beijing's hip, fashionable and discerning set always have a place to head to for excellent ambience, delicious drinks and five-star service.

THIS PAGE (FROM TOP): Choose from Centro's extensive drinks menu, and then lean back and enjoy; the very finest vintage is served at Centro, with reserves of 500 bottles in the well-stocked cellars.

OPPOSITE (CLOCKWSE FROM RIGHT): Start the evening on a high with this rosemary-garnished confection; the soft ambient lighting sets the mood for a hip, stylish night out; an afternoon rendezvous space.

SEATS
148

FOOD
bar menu

DRINK
extensive wine and cocktail list

FEATURES
live music • open 24 hours

NEARBY
Silk Street Market • Ritan Park •
Tuanjiehu Park

CONTACT
Kerry Centre Hotel, 1 Guanghua Road
Chaoyang District, Beijing 100020 •
telephone: +86.10.6561 8833 ext 42 •
facsimile: +86.10.6561 2626 •
email: hbkc@shangri-la.com •
website: www.shangri-la.com

the world of suzie wong

...the undisputed doyenne of Beijing's multi-hued club scene...

THIS PAGE: *An opulently upholstered daybed, one of many scattered around the club's lush premises.*

OPPOSITE (FROM TOP): *The antiques in The World of Suzie Wong boldly emphasise the Oriental interiors; a sumptuous palette of vivid red and orange prevails throughout.*

Having brought her stilettos, beautiful silks and all the mysterious charm of her former Hong Kong heyday with her, the seductive Suzie Wong appears to be alive and well today at the epicentre of the hottest nightlife in Beijing. The club, named after the 1957 novel by Richard Mason and subsequent film starring William Holden and Nancy Kwan, recreates the decadent opium dens and secretive retreats of 1930s Hong Kong in a beautiful, three-storied house.

The World of Suzie Wong first opened its doors and its arms in 2002, to the romance of the 'East meets West' storyline that ignites the turbulently passionate relationship in the film. Blending unabashedly opulent Eastern design—vibrant silks, rich-carved woods, delicate Chinese screens, low-lit embroidered lanterns—with the pulses and beats of the Western dance scene, The World of Suzie Wong has established itself as the undisputed doyenne of Beijing's

multi-hued club scene, drawing crowds of devotees to its doors and spawning a following of less successful copycat nightspots.

Decorated in lavish 1930s cabaret style, The World of Suzie Wong is an intricate, exotic blend of crimson decadence, mystery and sensuality. Dimly lit alcoves and curtained reclining beds clad in vivid silk and scattered with enticingly plump cushions provide little nooks for those in need of privacy, whilst several rooms, each throbbing and humming with a different genre of dance music, cater to the euphoria of the thronged crowd. Stone and rich hardwood floors bear the weight of thousands of eager clubbers; a delightfully rickety (but deceptively robust) staircase creaks under the burden of antique stone sculptures; Chinese lanterns cast an ambient velvety claret glow across the darkened rooms; Chinese screens create chill-out zones fortified with sumptuously inviting sofas; daybeds, gloriously replete in chinois chic, are found variously about the club, evocatively recalling Hong Kong's extinct vice dens of opium.

The main club area, with a strong Oriental theme of deep reds and oranges, is the pulsating cortex of the club, and by midnight, the strobe-lit dance floor is heaving with Beijing's well-heeled and fashionable international set. Upstairs, a generously furnished room caters to those needing a

THIS PAGE (FROM TOP): The club's VIP area is furnished in chinois chic; the original building structure is unadorned in some places for an authentic, classic 1930s effect.

OPPOSITE (FROM TOP): The bar, one of many in the club, is striking in a palette of Oriental red and gold; sumptuous details such as door mouldings and giant murals set the tone for nights of decadence; a vintage Victrola is nestled in a corner, a little dash of character.

breather from the dance floor, while still overlooking the action. For the ultimate chill out experience, an extensive outdoor terrace offers a welcome relaxation area with picturesque views of a moonlit Chaoyang Park. Bamboo walls, abundant flowers and luxuriant plants create a veritable bower in which to enjoy the gentle summer evening breeze. Throughout The World of Suzie Wong, multiple bars and attentive waiters ensure a constant supply of quenching beverages. The bars are ideal spots for people-watching, with a good view of the club interiors and long rows of tall barstools where one may nurse a drink and observe club denizens. Happy hours offer a wide range of house cocktails and an extensive wine list includes an impressive range of vintage wines sourced from a wide selection of vineyards worldwide.

FOOD
finger food

DRINKS
extensive wine list • cocktails

FEATURES
outdoor terrace • dance lounge •
opium beds • lounge

NEARBY
Sanlitun • Workers' Stadium •
Chaoyang Park

CONTACT
1A South Nongzhanguan Road
West Gate, Chaoyang Park
Chaoyang District, Beijing 100026 •
telephone: +86.10.6593 6049 •
facsimile: +86.10.6595 5049 •
email: clubsuziewong@263.net •
website: www.suziewong.com.cn

Offering an eclectic mix of jazz, salsa, hip hop, funk, Latino tunes and rousing house anthems, the music policy at The World of Suzie Wong is, above all, inclusive. Resident DJs Chozie and Bobby play each night alongside a stellar list of guest DJs and MCs from around the world. With growing international recognition of its merits, The World of Suzie Wong attracts an established and varied mix of DJs, ensuring its continued reputation for playing some of the best music in Beijing. The club also holds regular themed nights, where guests can expect to enjoy 60s grooves, Fantasy Nights, 80s disco, Cuban exotic and Summer Fiascos. Making the most out of any holiday or festival—read 'excuse to party'—The World of Suzie Wong hosts numerous events throughout the year, and for anyone keen to celebrate in style, it's guaranteed to be both the hottest and liveliest location for Christmas, New Year, Valentine's Day, and of course Suzie Wong's very own birthday anniversary. Attracting locals, expats and visitors from around the world, including Hollywood celebrities such as Colin Farrell, The World of Suzie Wong has become a key attraction in Beijing's nightlife, and after four years of wild partying still remains the club of choice for the capital's young and affluent crowd. To make the most of a night at The World of Suzie Wong, arrive early to enjoy sunset on the terrace before reserving an exclusive table in one of its many semi-private alcoves.

cottage boutique

...a veritable Aladdin's cave of little wonders and delights...

THIS PAGE (FROM TOP): The brightly painted walls set off the unusual pieces scattered about the shop; visitors who take the time to look through the myriad of items can find plenty of little hidden treats.
OPPOSITE (FROM TOP): Softly lit lamps and flowers give a homey feel; Cottage is aptly named for its cosy, domestic-inspired interiors; items for sale in the shop range from fine ceramics to jewellery.

Situated within a tiny artisan's enclave of galleries and picturesque cafés that looks out over Ritan Park, Cottage Boutique is a fascinating repository of treasures for the avid homemaker. Antique collectibles abound, interspersed with modern furniture creations, an eclectic mix of unique pieces that guarantees a fulfilling browsing experience for even the most jaded shopper. Nearby, the mega-malls of The Orchard and China World beckon with their bright lights and bustling crowds, but the quieter atmosphere and cosy intimacy of Cottage is a draw to those who wish for something a little further off the beaten track.

Cottage was named for its original location in a shop of just 20 sq m (215 sq ft), in the hub of Silk Street Market. Having moved to its current, larger space, Cottage retains its relaxed and welcoming atmosphere and is furnished to recall a stylish, contemporary home, with its vibrant colours, eye-catching pieces of furniture and gorgeously tactile fabrics. Reflecting the core themes of simplicity and comfort, the many lifestyle products found here include quirky one-of-a-kind gift items, jewellery, furnishings, hand-sewn cushions, table runners, candles, photo albums and Asian ceramics and pottery. Ranging from huge antique Chinese chests to modern abstract art, the assortment changes regularly and visitors can often find one-off pieces created by up-and-coming local designers as well as furniture from across China and Southeast Asia. Inspired by her passion for art, travel and film, owner Rebecca Hsu frequently travels across Asia and through the creative circles of Beijing for the products one finds at Cottage. For three months each year she trawls the remote regions of China, Thailand, Cambodia, Indonesia, the Philippines, Laos and Vietnam to find beautiful Southeast Asian antique furniture, restoring them to all their former glory. Involved in many music and art events in Beijing and even hosting her own contemporary art exhibition, Hsu promotes numerous young artists, and visitors to Cottage can also expect to see the latest designs currently making waves in Beijing's avant-garde scene sitting alongside the carved Tibetan chests, bright retro Chinese chairs and Thai figurines.

The shelves at Cottage are lined with all manner of finds for the patient browser; one is likely to lose hours examining the dazzling array. In this veritable Aladdin's cave of little wonders and delights, the visitor will be hard pressed not to walk away with bags bulging with a haul of purchases, from traditional tea sets to designer vases and fine china. Silk cushions, throws and table runners gleam like jewels displayed against surfaces of dark Asian woods. In fact, anything that has caught Hsu's eye on her travels through Asia can and will be found in their neat boxes and display cases, on the shelves and along the walls of her enchanting Cottage.

PRODUCTS
furniture • gifts • textiles • ceramics • jewellery

FEATURES
a diverse range of antique and modern lifestyle products

NEARBY
Ritan Park • The Orchard • Forbidden City • Tiananmen Square

CONTACTS
4 North Ritan Road
Chaoyang District, Beijing 100020 •
telephone: +86.10.8561 1517 •
email: rebecca0929@yahoo.com •

cottage warehouse

...beautifully restored chests, wardrobes, screens, chairs, tables, sculptures and more.

THIS PAGE: *The sheer range and variety of items on sale makes Cottage Warehouse the one-stop place to go for antiques.*

OPPOSITE: *From Asian statuettes to Oriental carved chairs and wall hangings, the shop has it all.*

Featuring a diverse and stunning selection of antique Asian furniture and contemporary artworks, Cottage Warehouse can be found in the heart of the commercial warehouse district to the southeast of central Beijing. Gathering precious artefacts from around Asia, owner Rebecca Hsu soon ran out of space at her boutique near Ritan Park and now uses this dramatic space to display the larger pieces of her impressive collection.

Spread over 2,400 sq m (26,000 sq ft) of warehouse, visitors can find hundreds of beautifully restored chests, wardrobes, screens, chairs, tables, sculptures and more. Covering all regions of China, including Shanxi, Shangdong, Zhejiang, Fujian, Gansu, Hebei and Tibet, Cottage Warehouse features one of the city's most impressive collection of Chinese antiques. From the small wooden washbasins to elaborately designed Tibetan chests, the sheer variety is remarkable and the warehouse has very quickly become the first, and often only, stop for those seeking authentic Chinese furniture in the Chinese capital.

Whilst primarily featuring Chinese antiques, Cottage Warehouse is also home to a variety of Asian furniture and artwork. For three months of the year, Hsu travels across Asia searching for interesting and unique pieces to bring back from Thailand, Cambodia, Indonesia, Philippines, Vietnam and Laos. Artefacts include bronze sculptures, medicine cabinets, daybeds and ceramics, all carefully restored in their turn. When the owner is on-site, make the most of her knowledge with a guided tour through the countless rows of furniture. Bubbling with enthusiasm, Hsu can recount the stories and history behind every piece.

Her passion extends beyond the past, and antique furniture—Hsu is an active member within the modern artistic scene of Beijing. Promoting many local designers and artists, the warehouse is also an outlet for some of the city's most radical design experiments. Funky chairs and ingeniously collapsible tables have been crafted from a variety of vibrant materials. These avant-garde pieces of furniture and contemporary artwork can be found amidst 200-year-old chests and traditional Chinese screens. The combination is an inspirational clash of traditional, lavish design and modern, minimalist elegance—a collaboration that would look great in any home. Throughout the year Cottage Warehouse hosts various events for art and design and on these rare occasions guests have the opportunity to meet the artists and view the exhibitions alongside the permanent displays.

Cottage Warehouse further offers a bespoke service allowing guests to design their own custom-made furniture. Replicating old or modern pieces and catering to individual designs they can guarantee a perfect fit for any cosy nooks standing empty in one's house.

PRODUCTS
Chinese and Asian antique and replicated furniture • modern designer furniture • contemporary artworks • bespoke furniture

FEATURES
regular events and exhibitions

CONTACT
for appointment: 4 North Ritan Road Chaoyang District, Beijing 100020 • telephone: +86.10.8561 1517 • email: rebecca0929@yahoo.com

rechenberg

...contemporary Parisian with an Asian twist and occasional Bavarian accents.

Right next to the smokestack of a disused residential heating plant, a steel door opens to reveal a green courtyard and a top-end fashion boutique-cum-atelier. Here, Kathrin von Rechenberg designs and sells her extensive range of tea silk and other natural fibre garments. The style is contemporary Parisian with an Asian twist and occasional Bavarian accents.

Munich born and bred, Kathrin first left her home city for Paris, to train as a designer. She then spent four years as a modelist and pattern-maker with various haute couture houses such as Jean-Louis Scherrer, Emanuelle Khan, Christian Dior, Christian Lacroix, and Chanel.

She soon became fascinated with a material which later became the basis for her own label—tea silk or xiangyun sha which means fragrant silk organdy. The fabric is handmade in a process consisting of 30 separate, delicate steps before it achieves its characteristic marbled gloss. Firstly, the material is dyed with vegetable juices, and subsequent steps involve covering the material with river sand and laying it out to dry naturally in the open air. The final step is a highly controlled process of washing the fabric in tea. If the resulting material is stored for several years before it is used, the sheen and quality improves markedly. For this reason, 'vintage' tea silk is traded in Japan just as a special wine vintage would be in the West.

THIS PAGE (FROM LEFT): The studio and boutique of Kathrin von Rechenberg is tucked away from the loud bustle of the city; items of clothing are displayed with an eye to clean, fluid lines; Kathrin specialises in the use of tea silk, with its distinctive moiré pattern and elegant dull sheen.

OPPOSITE: The range of clothing comes in a variety of materials for both men and women, while bespoke pieces such as formal wear can be made to order.

Kathrin has made tea silk the hallmark of her own fashion label. She also uses other fine fabrics such as wool, linen and cashmere. Her designs show her trademarks of elegant simplicity: flowing fabrics, clear lines and irreproachable cut. Classic suit jackets are made with wool crêpe georgette or velvet silk. Asian traditions can be clearly recognised among the details of her designs: wide kimono sleeves, Chinese-style band collars and wraparound trousers.

There is also a range of knitwear and a handful of accessories such as hand-dyed scarves and tea silk handbags available on the well-stocked shelves. Men like the tea silk shirts and jackets—style and elegance without the usual discomfort of formal clothes. Special items, such as cocktail dresses or ball gowns, can be made to measure. Kathrin presents her new collections twice a year at the exclusive Orchard restaurant on the outskirts of Beijing.

PRODUCTS
men's and women's fashion •
accessories

FEATURES
contemporary fusion style

NEARBY
north embassy district • Yu Yang Hotel

CONTACT
East Xinyuanxili Street
(yard behind Building 12)
Chaoyang District, Beijing 100027•
telephone: +86.10.6463 1788 •
facsimile: +86.10.6463 3995 •
email: info@rechenberg.cn •
website: www.rechenberg.cn

torana gallery

...own something beautiful, priceless and part of a rapidly vanishing way of life.

A passion for traditional Tibetan crafts and a fascination with the remote region of Tibet led Englishman Chris Buckley to establish Torana Gallery in 2000. With his first outlet located in Kempinski Hotel in Beijing, its success quickly led to a second store in Shanghai three years later.

Torana Gallery specialises in Tibetan textile crafts such as premium handmade rugs and carpets. The collection ranges from century-old tie-dyed saddle blankets to handwoven rugs with minimalist designs. Every new design combines modern simplicity with ancient Tibetan and Chinese motifs. Naturally dyed strands are woven into exquisitely detailed patterns which range from bold contemporary stripes to textured peonies.

Visitors to the gallery can also find antique carpets of classical Chinese, Mongolian, and Tibetan origins as well as original Khotan rugs with a distinct Middle-Eastern style. Selling only the top quality handmade carpets, Torana commissions most of the designs through its Tibetan workshop. However, Torana is also the exclusive distributor in China for Michaelian & Kohlberg carpets, which are handmade using traditional methods and wool from the Middle East.

Customers have the option of requesting for custom-made carpets and this service is often used by interior designers for luxury apartments and villas. Torana has also customised carpets for prominent corporate clients such as JP Morgan and McKinsey.

In Torana's workshops, the entire carpet-making process is painstakingly carried out by hand using traditional methods. The Tibetan carpets sold at Torana are made of one of the world's most expensive wool—pure Tibetan Highland wool. The strands are carded, spun, dyed and knotted by hand. This ensures that the fibres do not break and the carpets have a unique texture and are highly durable.

The carpets are made of natural and eco-friendly materials—wool pile with wool or unbleached cotton warp and weft. Hence, they contain no toxic substances and the manufacturing process produces very little waste, a consideration which is particularly important for the dry and fragile environment on the Tibetan plateau.

Torana also holds periodic fairs and exhibitions along Tibetan themes. These include contemporary thangka paintings, Tibetan art, antiques and photography. Carpets and rugs from Torana are guaranteed to last at least a lifetime. Using and promoting traditional Tibetan methods that have increasingly given way to production lines and modern technology, the gallery offers its customers the opportunity to own something beautiful, priceless and part of a rapidly vanishing way of life.

PRODUCTS
textiles • contemporary rugs •
antique Tibetan furniture •
hand-made carpets

FEATURES
shipping services • customised designs •
Tibetan art and photography exhibitions

NEARBY
Workers' Stadium • embassy district •
Sanlitun • Kempinski Hotel

CONTACT
Shop 8, Kempinski Hotel
50 Liangmaheqiao Road
Chaoyang District, Beijing 100016 •
telephone: +86.10.6465 3388
ext 5542 •
facsimile: +86.10.6465 3366 •
email: gallery@toranahouse.com •
website: www.toranahouse.com

central beijing

Beijing North Railway Station
Jishuitan
Xizhimen
Xizhimen
Andingmen
Guloudajie
Yonghegong
Lama Temple
Confucius Temple
Ghost Street
Dongzhimen
Dongzhimennei Avenue
Dongzhimen
Rear Lakes
Bell Tower
Drum Tower
Deshengmennei Avenue
Di'anmennwai Avenue
South Luogu Lane
West Di'anmen Avenue
East Di'anmen Avenue
Dongsishitiao
Nanxincang
Dongsishitiao
North Dongsi Avenue
Chegongzhuang
Beihai Park
White Dagoba
Jingshan Park
Chaoyangmennei Avenue
Chaoyangmen
Fuchengmen
Xi'anmen Avenue
> Chang + Biörck
> Garden of Delights
> Raffles Beijing Hotel
> Jaan
Forbidden City
Wangfujing Avenue
Dongsi Avenue
> Grand Hyatt Beijing
> Shanghai Tang
> My Humble House
> The Peninsula Beijing
> Red Gate Gallery
Dongdan
Jianguomennei Avenue
Jianguomen
Yonganli
Guomao
Financial Street
Nanlishilu
Fuxingmennei Avenue
West Chang'an Avenue
East Chang'an Avenue
Wangfujing
Ancient Observatory
Muxidi
Fuxingmen
Xidan
Tiananmenxi
Tiananmendong
Beijingzhan
Tiananmen Square
Dongjiaomin Lane
Beijing Railway Station
Qianmen
Xuanwumen
Dongjiaomin Lane
Qianmen Avenue
Qianmen
Chongwenmen
Ming Dynasty City Wall Ruins
Dongbianmen Watchtower
Changchunjie
Hepingmen
Qianmen
Liulichang Street
Guang'anmennei Avenue
Ox Street Mosque
Ox Street
Tiantan Road
Tiyuguan Road
Guang'anmen Railway Station
Yongdingmennwal Avenue
Temple of Heaven
East Tiantan Road
Beijing Amusement Park
Beijing South Railway Station

N

Legend

	Expressway
	Urban ring road
	Main road
	Other road
	Railway
	Railway station
	Light rail
	Subway
○	Subway/light rail station
○	Water

0 km   0.5   1   1.5   2 km

old peking

Central Beijing is the heart of old 'Peking', and traces of the city's colourful past can still be found here if you veer away from the main tourist district of Wangfujing Avenue. Dongcheng District, with its idyllic hutong (alleys) and many historical sights, is one of Beijing's nicest areas, and a few hours spent wandering around here will give you a better feeling for the city's past. Xicheng District, which abuts Dongcheng, is an eclectic hodgepodge of old hutong, courtyard houses, lakes and restaurants, with a bunch of historical sites mixed in between. The atmosphere in the southern part of Beijing, meanwhile, has a totally different feel. Prior to 1949, when the Communists took control of Beijing, this area was packed with small shops, old European architecture, Peking opera and acrobatic theatres, and street performers and magicians. Today, if you look hard enough, you will find a small part of this slice of the past still existing in the narrow lanes of the Chongwen and Xuanwu districts.

Although the urban spread has resulted in the demolition of many of the city's charming hutong and courtyard houses, the Chinese capital is starting to show a new appreciation for its proud past and rich heritage, renovating old temples, churches, courtyard houses, towers and parts of the old city wall.

THIS PAGE (FROM TOP): A bird's eye view of the Forbidden City; the door of a soon-to-be demolished courtyard house is covered by advertising stickers for moving companies.

OPPOSITE: A seemingly bemused Mao Zedong watches over Tiananmen Square.

PAGE 122: A girl strolls through the Forbidden City. In Beijing, the city's rich history is very much a part of everyday life.

a culture of lanes

For old-time residents of the capital, there is probably nothing more symbolic of the city than its idyllic, but rapidly disappearing, courtyard houses and twisting hutong, which one Chinese writer called a 'culture of lanes' and 'the soul of Beijing'. More than 20 hutong are today protected as historical sites.

No doubt, the best way to scratch the surface of this part of the city—before it disappears forever—is to take a trip through its hutong, past rows of courtyard houses.

The shortest hutong in Beijing is said to be just 25 m (82 ft) in length; the longest, 3 km (2 miles). No one seems to know exactly how many hutong there are, with estimates running between 1,300 and several thousand. According to one old Beijing saying: 'The major ones number 360; the small ones are as many as the number of hairs on an ox.' In other words, there are more than one can count.

It is known, however, that hutong have been around for more than 700 years, dating back to the Yuan Dynasty (1271–1368), when Kublai Khan had his capital at Dadu, the site of present-day Beijing. In fact, the word 'hutong' is believed to have derived from the Mongolian word 'hong tong', which means 'water well'.

One of the most interesting things about hutong is their names. During imperial days, there were no signs marking the hutong, whose names were only passed on

orally. It was not until the 1911 revolution that street signs were nailed to the walls. Some are named after national heroes, some for their geographical location, and others for the trades that once prospered on these streets. Hence, one might find Cotton Hutong, Rice Hutong, Vegetable Hutong, Tea Leaf Hutong and Great Li's Hat Hutong. Some names are purely descriptive; Little Horn Hutong is thus named because one end is much wider than the other end. This is one of the smallest hutong in the city, stretching just 0.6 m (2 ft) at its narrow end, and accommodating only one bicycle at a time.

Peek inside a courtyard door and you will likely see dozens of potted plants, and perhaps the morning's vegetable shopping: a long string of entwined garlic bulbs hanging from a wall alongside strands of red peppers. Cabbages, onions, string beans, winter melons and eggplants sit on a windowsill. In the corner is a neat pile of

THIS PAGE: The golden roofscape of the Forbidden City seen from a pavilion atop Jingshan Park.

OPPOSITE (FROM TOP): A narrow passageway hidden in a corner of the old imperial city; a shaded area in a traditional courtyard house, a way of living fast making way for 'urban renewal' in the Chinese capital.

honeycomb-like coal briquettes used for heating the house in the winter. Architectural details, which can still be seen today, whisper secrets about the former owners of these once grand complexes. In the past, there was a strict hierarchy that dictated the architectural style of one's home, with the symbols on the front of each house describing the owner's rank and social status. Homes with elaborate Chinese-style gates and spreading eaves were often the former residences of imperial officials or wealthy businessmen, while the homes of commoners would have simple square-topped gates; these were referred to as the 'eagle will not alight' gates.

Above the doorway of each house are either two or four lintels, often carved with auspicious Chinese characters. Common families would have two lintels; wealthy or official ones, four. A typical phrase on lintels will have the characters 'ru yi', or 'as you wish'. Some modern ones simply say 'revolution'. Wealthy homes also usually have decorative door clasps, cymbal-shaped doorknockers, and protective brass wrappings, often in the shape of a pomegranate, a symbol of fertility and many offspring.

The carved stone drums that sit on each side of the door of a courtyard house also indicate something about the status of the family living within. Royalty would be identified by dragons; common people, by

THIS PAGE (FROM TOP): An imperial red door, above which are four lintels, opens to a courtyard; a pride of lions, symbolising power and believed to offer protection from evil spirits, stand guard in the Forbidden City.

OPPOSITE: A poster of actress Ingrid Bergman is all that remains from a courtyard house that has been demolished in the Qianmen section of Beijing.

artistic designs; and the poor, by a very small stone. These decorated stones support the door axle, and are also believed to repel ghosts and attract good fortune. Some of these houses have intricate overhead brick carvings along their walls: lions were used for the homes of military generals; elephants for civil officials; and plums, orchids and bamboo for scholars.

One good way to gain a leisurely close-up view of the insides of these houses is by visiting one of the restored homes of well-known past residents of the city. Many of these houses have been turned into museums. They are also an important part of the city's cultural history, providing inspiration to famous writers such as Lu Xun, Lao She and Mao Dun, and painters Qi Baishi and Xu Beihong, who all lived in beautiful Beijing courtyard houses. 'Without the hutong, modern Chinese literature in China would only have been half as significant as it has been,' wrote one writer.

The poor conditions in many hutong explain why many residents are keen to move into modern high rises. Few courtyard houses have gas for heating or cooking, and many do not even have toilets, which is why there are so many public toilets interspersed between the houses. At daybreak, it is common to see people—night pans in hand—coming out of their courtyard houses and heading to neighbourhood toilets.

tiananmen square

Tiananmen Square can be considered the political centre of modern China. During the Ming and Qing Dynasties, this used to be a public gathering place, and after the fall of imperial rule, the area was to play host to repeated political demonstrations.

University students came here to protest against Japanese demands on China in 1919, emotional Red Guards held rallies here during the Cultural Revolution (1966–76), and a million people gathered here in 1976 to mourn the passing of Premier Zhou Enlai. Several months later, Mao Zedong passed away, and thousands of labourers worked frantically to complete the construction of the Chairman Mao Memorial Hall at the rear of the square to house the remains of the man who had led China for some five decades.

Stand at the front of the square looking north at the Gate of Heavenly Peace and you will see a large portrait of Chairman Mao smiling down upon those below—almost benevolently. It was from the rostrum of the Gate of Heavenly Peace that the Great Helmsman declared the establishment of the People's Republic of China in October 1949.

In the middle of the square is the Monument to the People's Heroes, a 36-m (118-ft) obelisk that memorialises those who gave their lives for the revolution. Bas-reliefs around the monument depict famous scenes from modern Chinese history. Just behind the monument is the Chairman Mao Memorial Hall. After Mao's death, Party leaders overruled his wish to be cremated and had his body embalmed and placed here. Guards see to it that visitors to the hall are kept moving at a fast pace while they pass by the crystal coffin.

On the west side of the square is the Great Hall of the People, where the National People's Congress meets. On the east side is the National Museum of China, home to a collection of more than 610,000 artefacts. At the southern end, the Zhengyang Gate has a decent showcase of ancient bronze mirrors and photographs of old Beijing gates. Just south of this imperial structure is the outer gate, known as the Arrow Tower.

East of the Great Hall of the People, facing Chang'an Avenue, is the highly controversial National Grand Theater—people tend to either hate it or love it. The building, which looks like a modernistic flying saucer, was designed by

THESE TWO PAGES: The magnificent Forbidden City is often the first stop on the itinerary for most visitors to the Chinese capital.

The theatre's futuristic design has aroused the ire of critics...

Paul Andreu and features the French architect's sleek titanium and glass-dome design, giving viewers the impression that the structure is floating on water. People entering the complex will have to board escalators to the lobby, passing under a water tunnel. The theatre's futuristic design has aroused the ire of critics who deem it out of place, being as close as it is to so many imperial structures. This, however, is a criticism that could also be made about the Soviet-style architecture surrounding the square.

forbidden city

Dating back some six centuries, the Forbidden City now boasts China's most complete array of imperial architecture. More than 200,000 workers and craftsmen worked on this sprawling site, which housed a long line of imperial leaders, beginning with Yongle in 1420. Pu Yi, the last emperor, made known around the world through Bernardo Bertolucci's classic film, remained in this palace until a warlord forced him to vacate it in 1924. After walking through the Forbidden City, visitors can enjoy a bird's eye view of this magnificent complex by heading to Jingshan (Prospect Hill) Park opposite the north gate, and hiking to the Pavilion of Everlasting Spring on the top of the hill.

playground of the imperial family

Beihai Park is a perennial favourite with Beijing families who come here to boat and stroll in the summer, and for a turn around the frozen lake in the winter. But it was once the romping grounds of the imperial court for centuries, and also the home of Mao Zedong's wife, Jiang Qing. The Liao Dynasty (907–1125) constructed an imperial palace here, to which succeeding dynasties added hills, water features, pavilions, and more buildings; they even launched a makeover of the park. In the Ming Dynasty, a road was built over the centre of the lake, dividing it into northern and southern lakes.

THIS PAGE: The broad, elegant curves of the Forbidden City's Inner Golden River.

OPPOSITE: A worker sweeps the grounds of the new—and controversial—National Grand Theater. Critics say the French-designed futuristic building, also known as 'The Egg', is out of place among the ancient structures in the area.

At the south entrance to the park is the Circular City. Important here is the Hall of Receiving Light, which houses a 4.5-m (15-ft) white jade Buddha, alleged to have been a gift from Burma to Empress Dowager Cixi. In the courtyard is a huge jade basin sitting on a jade pedestal, which Kublai Khan is believed to have used as a sort of imperial punch bowl during official banquets.

Just to the north of the Circular City is Qionghua Islet. Beihai Park's unmistakable landmark—the 36-m- (119-ft-) high White Dagoba Temple—was placed here in 1651 when the Dalai Lama visited Beijing. A short walk away, on the south side of the islet facing the lakefront, is Fangshan, a restaurant serving imperial cuisine.

the rear lakes

The beauty of the Rear Lakes has been badly affected by the runaway economic development of the area, which has seen a bevy of bars and restaurants take lakefront spots around a good portion of the lake. Once a quiet place for an evening stroll, the area today is a gauntlet of masseuses, bar touts, cars, pedicab drivers and huge crowds on the weekends. Still, if one takes the time to wander off the main road running along the lake, it's possible to find some excellent examples of old architecture and traditional life in the alleys just off the waterfront.

Despite the changes going on around the city, to a certain extent, time seems to have stood still in these busy hutong. Walk down the street and you're likely to see a small shop hawking Muslim snacks, or a stand selling steamed meat buns, the cooks disappearing behind a thick cloud of steam. Throughout the day, peddlers push their wheel carts down the street, shouting out the names of their wares, some chanting well-known rhymes to advertise their products.

At one corner, schoolboys crowd around an old man with dozens of small woven baskets—each the size of a plum—spread before him on the sidewalk. Inside are crickets or grasshoppers. Some other children are playing kanbao, a traditional Chinese game in which a small sand-filled bag is kicked back and forth. A few boys

THIS PAGE (FROM TOP): Man waiting for a catch on the Rear Lakes; a swimmer takes a dip in the icy lake on a cold winter day.
OPPOSITE: Lotus plants on the water of Beijing's Rear Lakes.

...a quiet place for an evening stroll...

kick around a soccer ball. Turn the corner and you'll likely see a gaggle of grandmothers sitting on short stools in front of their houses, some looking after grandchildren, others dozing off in the noon-day sun. One housewife comes out of her house, a basket of wet laundry in her hand, which she hangs on a wash line in front of her house.

Beside the Rear Lakes, elderly Beijing residents are absorbed in the same pastimes their ancestors enjoyed more than 100 years ago, from a simple game of Chinese chess to mahjong. The latter, banned during the puritanical heyday of Communist rule, has made a strong comeback, with the sound of clicking tiles increasingly heard coming from small shops in the hutong. This is also a good place to enjoy traditional snacks sold by itinerant food vendors, but don't wait too long. Like the hutong, these old favourites are fading fast. Take a stroll around the lake and you'll probably chance upon the sweet-potato man, who has turned his tricycle into a restaurant on the go. A used oil drum, balanced between the two rear wheels, serves as a baking unit. Small briquettes of coal are fed into an opening at the bottom of the drum, which roasts the sweet potatoes strung around the top rim. In winter, a popular treat is the candied haw. As many as nine pieces of this small red fruit, which resemble miniature apples, are strung on a small wooden stick and are then dipped into boiling candy liquid. The colder the weather, the crispier the candy coating.

an ancient alleyway comes back to life

South Luogu Lane, a long and busy hutong lined with interesting Republican-era architecture, is fast becoming a new drinking, dining and shopping mecca in Beijing. The quaint coffee shops set up in these old buildings with their skylights and large windows all offer wi-fi, and are a magnet for the growing number of laptop-toting Chinese and foreigners in search of free cyber-surfing during the day. In the evening, this is also a popular venue for drinks, desserts or a chat with friends. The best thing is

that none of the Rear Lake's touts have found their way to the street yet. With its long history, South Luogu Lane is also a great place for exploring the surrounding alleyways.

marching to a new beat

Throughout history, drum and bell towers have been an important part of daily and official life in Chinese cities. Constructed in 1420, Beijing's Drum Tower (directly north of Prospect Hill) used to house 24 drums, which announced the

THIS PAGE (FROM TOP): The square in front of the Bell Tower; the growing number of new businesses on South Luogu Lane has given the old alleyway a new lease of life.

OPPOSITE: Tourists stroll around the grounds of the home of Prince Gong, one of the best preserved aristocratic mansions remaining from the Qing Dynasty.

night watches; today, only one remains, although 24 new drums are still sounded half-hourly for the enjoyment of tourists. Opposite this structure is the imposing Bell Tower—a 33-m- (108-ft-) high brick structure. Its enormous bronze bell can be heard from 20 km (12 miles) away, and used to be rung daily at 7 p.m. until Pu Yi, the last emperor, was chased out of the Forbidden City in 1924. The two tall towers provide interesting vistas of the hutong below, which are in a historic part of the old capital.

old temples

Known for its religious and political significance during the Qing Dynasty, with an estimated 1,500 Tibetan, Mongol and Chinese lamas living here, the Lama Temple is also famous for being the former residence of Emperor Yongzheng. The complex was converted into a Tibetan temple upon his taking reign in 1723, and was later used by the Yellow Hat sect of Tibetan Buddhism (popularly known as Lamaism) as an institution of learning. Although the Lama Temple was ruined during the Cultural Revolution, the buildings were reputedly saved when Premier Zhou Enlai intervened and stopped rampaging Red Guards from destroying them.

First built in the 13th century, the Confucius Temple—second in size only to the Confucius Temple in Qufu (the great sage's hometown in Shandong province)—was renovated in the 18th century, and more recently in 2007. Visitors will find a serene courtyard full of cypress and pine trees, and 189 steles carrying the names and birthplaces of those who aced the imperial exams from 1416 to 1904, the last year the exam was given. Carved stone drums, made during the Qianlong (1736–96) period, flank the two sides of the Great Accomplishment Gate. During imperial times, emperors and court officials visited the temple to make offerings to Confucius; today, students come here every year before the national university entrance exam to burn incense to the old master, in return for help in the examination. The temple was ruined by young Red Guards during the Cultural Revolution when Confucianism was deemed a symbol of feudalism. However, a Confucian revival kicked off in the mid-1990s, and it's now enjoying a new-found popularity.

the old granaries

Nanxincang, China's oldest existing granary dating back to the Yongle period (1403–24), is now one of Beijing's hottest entertainment venues and is home to three art galleries, a bookshop, a teahouse, and a number of bars and restaurants. It was once among the 300-odd granaries that operated in this neighbourhood during

THIS PAGE (FROM TOP): The Confucius Temple is dedicated to China's great sage, who is making a big comeback across China; worshippers at the Lama Temple brave the flames shooting out from an incense burner.
OPPOSITE: Incense smoke and its pungent smell fill the air at the bustling Lama Temple.

imperial days; sadly, all of the granaries, except for Nanxincang, have disappeared since then. The structures at this significant historical site are a mere 10 years younger than those of the Forbidden City.

Grain storage was extremely well thought-out in imperial China. Yicang were grain storage places for common people, while guancang served officials and the military, who were paid in grain for their services. The granaries were all built according to conventionalised standards, and the floors were paved with thick bricks and covered with wooden boards resting on brick shoulders to insulate the grain from the moisture of the earth. An elevated opening in the centre of the roof, which can still be seen today, was enclosed with woven bamboo strips to prevent birds from entering, but still provided sufficient ventilation. The 1.5-m- (5-ft-) thick walls stabilised the room temperature and prevented the grain from getting mouldy.

Grain was shipped north along the 4,828-km- (3,000-mile-) long Grand Canal system linking Hangzhou and Tongzhou (present day Tongxian). From Tongzhou, the grain travelled by cart to Chaoyang Gate, or the Gate Facing the Sun. It was from here that the grain was then delivered to the Forbidden City, and also distributed to the various granaries scattered near the gate.

beijing's wall street

To the far west of Xicheng is Financial Street—Beijing's answer to New York City's Wall Street. This area sprang up seemingly overnight, but is already home to a number of Chinese and international financial institutions. Many shops, restaurants and bars, as well as some of Beijing's poshest new five-star hotels, are following the bankers to this area, which is the new face of modern China.

chongwen and xuanwu

The two districts to the south—Chongwen and Xuanwu—have some of the oldest neighbourhoods in the city. Qianmen Avenue, the street running directly south of Tiananmen Square, has long been a bustling shopping area, with many traditional shops and restaurants, including many laozihao (old brand name shops), some dating back more than a century, still doing business here. The Ruifuxiang Silk Shop, which first opened its doors for business in 1893, has bolts of cloth stacked on its shelves, displaying a wide variety of colourful fabric, including silk, cotton, cashmere and wool. Choose the type you want and the shop clerk will cut yards of cloth from heavy bolts.

Around Qianmen, hawker stands and restaurants spill out on to the sidewalk, while people, cars and bicycles fight for a free piece of space to negotiate their way down the warren of narrow streets criss-crossing this neighbourhood. Enter any hutong and you'll find yourself immediately rubbing elbows—and a bit more—with other shoppers.

THIS PAGE: *A billboard covering a dilapidated part of the old Qianmen area hints at what to expect after the renovation.*

OPPOSITE (FROM TOP): *Nanxincang, the last remaining Ming granary, is overshadowed by the New Poly Plaza, one of Beijing's slickest new high rises; a couple walks by an advertisement promoting a new commercial property.*

And yet, at the same time, the neighbourhood is undergoing a huge renovation that has seen many old buildings—and entire streets—disappear. No one knows if the remake will successfully capture the authentic feel of the old street; previous attempts to re-create history have met with very uneven results.

Just to the west of here is Liulichang Street, Beijing's old art street, where the Ming and Qing Dynasty literati used to shop for rice paper, calligraphy brushes, ink stones, art, antiques and other items. The street today continues to sell many of these items, and remains a fun place to explore, despite having been turned into what looks like a touristy and unrealistic set for an old Chinese movie.

the old legation

Despite China's efforts to keep foreigners at a distance, foreign governments began opening embassies and consulates along Dongjiaomin Lane after China lost the Second Opium War (1856–60) with the British and French. Prior to this, the area had been home to tributary missions from Vietnam, Korea and Burma. Over the years, a number of foreign banks and other businesses opened in the foreign enclave, and a wall went up around the area. During the Boxer Rebellion of 1900, the Legation Quarter was under attack from the Boxers, also known as the Society of Harmonious Fists, for close to two months until the Eight Nation Alliance arrived to lift the siege. The Legation Quarter continued to serve as an embassy area after liberation and up until 1959, when the embassies moved northeast of here.

Dongjiaomin Lane is today a pale shadow of its former self. However, there is a surprising amount of European architecture dating back to that period, although in some instances you may have to peek over walls or through cracks to see what's survived. Most interesting are St. Michael's (the old French Catholic Church), the Yokohama Species Bank, and the former City Bank of New York.

There are big plans for one corner of the old Legation Quarter. Chinese-American property developer Handel Lee—one of the main forces behind Xintiandi and Three on

the Bund in Shanghai—is planning to turn the century-old former US Embassy into an upmarket entertainment and shopping venue. The complex is expected to open in 2007 and will include a branch of the Michelin three-star Enoteca Pinchiorri; two restaurants from Hong Kong's Aqua Restaurant Group; and a spin-off of Lee's former Beijing restaurant RBL. Besides these dining venues, the complex will also house a series of glass-and-marble buildings, which will accommodate a 140-seat repertory theatre, art gallery, café, and venues for such events as open-air jazz concerts.

ming dynasty city wall ruins and the watchtower

The new Ming Dynasty City Wall Ruins Park running along East Chongwenmen Avenue is a section of Beijing's old inner city wall. The structure was rebuilt using original bricks that had been snatched decades earlier after the city wall had been torn down. It is now a nicely landscaped area with paths full of Chinese walking their dogs, flying kites, practising martial arts, and playing with their children. On the eastern end of the

THIS PAGE: The imposing Dongbianmen Watchtower.

OPPOSITE (FROM TOP): A set of calligraphy brushes hangs in an art shop on Liulichang Street; a turn-of-the-century colonial building sits along the former Legation Quarter, once home to foreign embassies and banks.

ruins is the grand Dongbianmen Watchtower, the last remaining Ming Dynasty watchtower in the city. The tower is now home to the popular Red Gate Gallery on the first level and an interesting museum devoted to the history of the Chongwen District on the upper floors. Red Gate Gallery, which displays works by famous contemporary Chinese artists, was set up in 1991 by Brian Wallace, an Australian who studied art history at China's Central Academy of Fine Arts.

the temple of heaven

One of the finest examples of religious architecture remaining in China today, the Temple of Heaven began to be built in 1406 during the Yongle period, and took 14 years to complete. This sacred site was where the 'Son of Heaven' (as the emperor was known) would offer prayers and sacrifices during the winter solstice for a good harvest. He would fast for three days before the rituals began, and on the day before the ceremony, he would be carried on a palanquin out of the Forbidden City to fast overnight in the Hall of Abstinence, while the people of Beijing remained indoors and kept quiet throughout the long procession. Imperial sacrifices at the Hall of Prayer for Good Harvests were last offered in 1914 by Yuan Shikai—the ambitious president of the new republic, and an emperor wannabe.

ox street muslim quarter

Urban 'renewal' has destroyed the bulk of the city's old Muslim Quarter, an area that has been home to the Muslim community for more than 1,000 years. The sole survivor is the Ox Street Mosque, which was first erected in 996 and which, like other mosques in China, looks like a traditional Buddhist temple. It is usually crowded with the faithful who come here to pray. The Tower for Observing the Moon and the main hall are restricted areas, and women can only visit certain sections of the mosque. A few Muslim shops—primarily halal restaurants and butchers—still line the sidewalks here, now dwarfed by new and tall apartment complexes.

THIS PAGE: A group of Chinese Muslims prepares to pray at the Ox Street Mosque, in Beijing's Muslim quarter, at the end of Ramadan. A mosque first appeared on this site in 996.

OPPOSITE: The Hall of Prayer for Good Harvests at the Temple of Heaven, one of the best examples of religious architecture in China today.

One of the finest examples of religious architecture remaining in China today...

grand hyatt beijing

...unique ambience which is ideal for relaxation.

THIS PAGE (FROM TOP): *The Grand Suite displays the impeccable style shown throughout the hotel; the coffee bar is located in the residence, a sophisticated venue and an ideal place for high-profile cocktail receptions, product launches and glamorous social occasions.*

OPPOSITE (CLOCKWISE FROM TOP LEFT): *A fully equipped Diplomatic Suite; guests can luxuriate in the resort-style indoor pool with piped-in underwater music; the warm ambience of the hotel lobby beckons invitingly; an elegant décor sets the mood for the evening at Made in China.*

Atop China's largest shopping complex, Oriental Plaza, and only a short walk from Beijing's Forbidden City, the Grand Hyatt lays claim to the ultimate location in town. Set in the centre of Beijing's business and commercial district, it has become an ideal base for business and leisure travellers alike. Within the prestigious Oriental Plaza, some 120,000 sq m (1.3 million sq ft) are dedicated to boutiques, cafés and restaurants in one of the most popular shopping destinations in the capital. A short walk through the picturesque Changpu River Park leads to the city's major attractions which include Tiananmen Square, Temple of Heaven and Wangfujing shopping street.

The spacious interior is flooded with light, and full-length windows throughout the hotel offer impressive views of the city. Blending Western and Asian influences, guestrooms are stylishly simple with rich woods, crisp white linens, suede sofas and artwork from local and Asian artists. Deluxe rooms offer a separate dining and living area with a kitchenette and private bar. For added decadence, the Grand Hyatt's Diplomatic Suites are fully equipped apartments with a spacious living area and even include a 107-cm (42-in) flat-screen

television, DVD, CD and MP3 players, and an in-room fax. A suite butler is on hand to unpack luggage and order drinks while one can enjoy the unparalleled views from the floor-to-ceiling windows overlooking the Forbidden City.

The star attraction of the fully equipped fitness centre is a stunning resort-style indoor pool which stretches between Roman pillars and palm trees. Replete with multiple jacuzzis,

underwater music and a virtual sky featuring different weather patterns, the pool has a unique ambience which is ideal for relaxation. Surrounding the pool area, a lush tropical landscape conceals a gym and spa. To meet the needs of its business travellers, the hotel has dedicated nearly 3,000 sq m (32,292 sq ft) to meeting rooms, conference facilities and a majestic ballroom offering the latest technology.

With plenty of restaurants and bars around the Grand Hyatt, there is no shortage of options for evening entertainment. Within the hotel itself, visitors can also find delectable cuisine and a lively atmosphere. Redmoon, popular for its sushi-style lunches and evening cocktails, creates a sexy underground retreat with its blazing fire, red sofas and wine cellar. Made In China's contemporary décor, which features full-length windows, brick walls and an

open kitchen, reflects the modern slant on Chinese specialities such as Peking Duck and Beggar's Chicken. At Noble Court, diners can enjoy a more traditional fare of classic Cantonese cuisine alongside signature dishes such as Succulent Pork Ribs Flavoured with Coffee. The Grand Café combines a variety of Western and Asian flavours in its show kitchen, and for traditional Italian fare, Da Giorgio has created an intimate bistro atmosphere with lovely views across the green-tiled roofs of a traditional courtyard house.

ROOMS
825

FOOD
Made In China: northern Chinese • Noble Court: Cantonese • Redmoon: international • The Patisserie: pastries • Grand Café: international • Da Giorgio: Italian

DRINK
Redmoon • Fountain Lounge

FEATURES
24-hour fitness centre • resort-style indoor pool • spa • limousine service • ballroom • business centre • 24-hour concierge • wireless Internet access

NEARBY
Forbidden City • Tiananmen Square • Temple of Heaven • Great Wall

CONTACT
Beijing Oriental Plaza
1 East Chang'an Avenue,
Dongcheng District, Beijing 100738 •
telephone: +86.10.8518 1234 •
facsimile: +86.10.8518 0000 •
email: grandhyattbeijing@hyattintl.com •
website: www.beijing.grand.hyatt.com

raffles beijing hotel

...the centre of Beijing's cultural and entertainment scene for close to a century.

THIS PAGE (FROM TOP): *The hotel's welcoming lobby is resplendent in high arches and chandeliers; the Drawing Room in soothing tones of brown and light cream; the luxurious Grand Hotel Suite Living Room at Raffles Beijing.*

OPPOSITE (CLOCKWISE FROM TOP): *Little artistic touches set the mood; enjoy an elegant tea at La Vie; the hotel façade glows at night; a fine dining experience awaits.*

Opened in 1917, Raffles Beijing Hotel has been the centre of Beijing's cultural and entertainment scene for close to a century. Over the years, it has played a significant role in the capital's cultural events, hosting many local and foreign dignitaries including Dr Sun Yat Sen, General Zhang Xueliang and Charles de Gaulle. After a year of extensive renovations, Raffles Beijing Hotel has now reopened its doors to a new generation of businessmen and travellers.

The hotel's colonial charm, for which it is famed, remains largely intact, with huge brass handled doors, vaulted arches, sweeping hallways, inlaid marble and polished timber floors. French elegance is deftly combined with Oriental splendour in each of the 171 glamorous guestrooms. Elaborate white dressing tables sit alongside antique Chinese wood chests and grand European lamps glow softly through the traditional Chinese screens. Enormous beds dressed in quality linen ensure a good night's sleep whilst in the bathroom, an oversized bath and invigorating rain-shower guarantee a totally refreshed body. For a truly decadent stay in

China's historic capital, five stately suites, over 155 sq m (1,670 sq ft) in size, feature four-poster-beds, chaise longues and beautiful antique Chinese rugs.

Within the hotel, two distinctive restaurants indulge all Eastern and Western cravings. Inspired by the hotel's colonial past, Jaan takes guests back to the heyday of China in the 1920s while serving modern French cuisine. East 33 blends Chinese and Italian influences for everything from rustic wood-fired pizzas to crispy Peking Duck. The open-plan kitchen and contemporary style—the waiters all wear colourful mod 1960s glasses—create a fun and casual setting for breakfast, lunch or dinner.

Honouring many Chinese and foreign literati who have resided at the hotel, including dramatist George Bernard Shaw, American journalist Edgar Snow, and French photojournalist Henri Cartier-Bresson, The Writers Bar is an intimate den for cocktails and cigars. Reviving the grand tradition of afternoon tea, La Vie presents freshly made sandwiches and pastries on the finest ebony china. Situated at the crossroads of the famous Chang'an Avenue and Wangfujing Avenue, the hotel and its array of fine dining and colonial drinking holes is located in the heart of the business and commercial district.

ROOMS
171

FOOD
Jaan: French • East 33: Chinese and Italian

DRINK
Writers Bar • La Vie: tea lounge

FEATURES
indoor pool • business centre • limousine service

NEARBY
Tiananmen Square • Silk Street Market • Forbidden City

CONTACT
33 East Chang'an Avenue, Dongcheng District, Beijing 100004 • telephone: +86.10.6526 3388 • facsimile: +86.10.8500 4380 • email: beijing@raffles.com • website: www.beijing.raffles.com

the peninsula beijing

...the one hotel in Beijing that has it all...

When one is pressed to name the one hotel in Beijing that has it all, among yet above all the starred hotels and properties in the bustling city, the answer inevitably points to The Peninsula Beijing. Rising from the thoroughfares of Wangfujing and its gleaming retail palaces, The Peninsula Beijing offers elegance and high luxury housed within an exquisite blend of smooth modern architecture with traditional Chinese elements.

THIS PAGE (FROM RIGHT): Rooms at The Peninsula Beijing are modern, with traditional Chinese touches shown in the fabrics and accents; the living room of the Peninsula Suite is an exercise in luxury.

OPPOSITE (FROM TOP): The heated indoor pool caters to the active; a spectacular view of the hotel's grand exterior as the night falls; JING, the New Asian restaurant with a shining list of accolades.

Guests stepping into the hotel lobby will find themselves in a warm, tranquil space with courteously solicitous staff on hand to see to every comfort, a welcome respite from the cacophony of the metropolis beyond the hotel doors. The Peninsula Beijing is particularly renowned for its exemplary levels of service, a reputation that is immediately apparent from the second one is greeted by a smiling concierge, bags discreetly and efficiently moved upstairs to the rooms by soberly clad bellboys.

The hotel has a total of 525 guestrooms, including 57 suites and the magnificent signature Peninsula Suite. This grand suite of rooms consists of 60 sq m (660 sq ft) of pure indulgence, with a private lift and a separate dining room for 18 guests. Complimentary high-speed Internet access is standard in all rooms, as are flat screen televisions, CD and DVD players, separate sitting and sleeping areas, and deluxe marble bathrooms.

Part of The Peninsula Beijing's recent US$35 million makeover is the arrival on the scene of its remodeled state-of-the-art facilities and new award-winning restaurants. JING, voted one of the '75 Hottest Tables in the world' by *Condé Nast Traveler* (USA) features a wildly successful meld of western cuisine and culinary techniques with the delicate strength of Asian flavours. This shrine of New Asian gastronomy is open for breakfast, lunch and dinner, with

semi-private and private rooms available so guests may indulge themselves in a whole range of dining experiences. Also within the building is Huang Ting, bastion of traditional dim sum and authentic Cantonese or Beijing specialities, housed in a space built to recall a noble courtyard house from the olden days of imperial China. The Lobby on the other hand is popular for cocktails and coffee, and serves the signature Peninsula afternoon tea.

After a surfeit of the toothsome delights on offer at the restaurants, guests may repair to the spa and health club to enjoy the benefits of the available massages and sundry treatments. An indoor heated pool and fully equipped gym cater to the active, with sauna and steam rooms to wind down in. The fashionably inclined may choose to head to The Peninsula Arcade, lined with prestigious single-brand boutiques such as Givenchy, Dior, Kenzo, and—for those who like some sparkle in their life—Harry Winston and Cartier.

With such an array of distractions within and without their rooms, guests may be forgiven for feeling torn between staying in an exploring all the fine facilities that the hotel has to offer. It would be a shame not to venture out into the dazzling city for the duration of one's stay, especially with the proximity of some of Beijing's most enduring attractions, but those who wish to do so will find everything they need right in The Peninsula Beijing.

ROOMS
525

FOOD
JING: New Asia • Huang Ting: dim sum, Cantonese and Beijing • The Lobby: afternoon tea

DRINK
The Lobby

FEATURES
The Peninsula Arcade • spa and health club • indoor heated pool • gym • sauna and steam rooms • massage • chauffeur service • event and meeting facilities • complimentary wireless and wired Internet access • MP3/MP4 connectivity • off-premises catering

NEARBY
shopping district • Forbidden City • Tiananmen Square

CONTACT
8 Goldfish Lane, Wangfujing Dongcheng District, Beijing 100006 • telephone: +86.10.8516 2888 • facsimile: +86.10.6510 6311 • email: pbj@peninsula.com • website: beijing.peninsula.com

garden of delights

...a dining experience from half a world away.

Down the road from Beijing's iconic Forbidden City, the Garden of Delights is an entrée into a dining experience from half a world away. In fact, the space was inspired by the 15th-century religious masterpiece 'Garden of Earthly Delights' by prolific Dutch painter Hieronymus Bosch.

The result is a décor that is both modern yet with a touch of old-world charm. The experience begins with a setting dotted with oversized white pots of leafy fronds, exposed brick walls, smooth wooden floors and discreet custom-made Palm Trees Macetas motifs similar to those found in Latin America. Architect and interior designer Antonio Ochoa has created a space that is entirely fresh, filled with a light, contemporary energy. The Garden's design highlight is an elegant timber-girded vaulted ceiling intercut with skylights, that runs the entire length of the warm and intimate dining room.

Internationally acclaimed Venezuelan chef Edgar Leal has introduced to the Chinese capital a delightful ensemble of contemporary Latin American cuisine such as Cuban Black Bean Foam, Venezuelan Cixi Pepiada, Tamale with Seafood, Chicken smothered with Mexican Mole Sauce and a delightful Argentinean Matambre with Red Wine Sauce. A wide range of preferences have thoughtfully been taken into consideration, and equally, if not more so, delicious vegetarian options of set lunches are also available.

Furthermore, given that chocolate was first made known to the world via the intrepid explorers of the New World, it's appropriate that the Garden of Delights also makes a splash with its impressive range of chocolate desserts.

Meanwhile, over at the bar—an ideal spot for an intimate tête à tête or a post-prandial aperitif—Chef Leal serves up a spread of wildly

THIS PAGE (FROM LEFT): A wide range of fine wines fully complements all that the menu has to offer; enjoy a well-made cocktail at the bar before or after a meal; the classic ceviche dish is given a stylish, contemporary update.

OPPOSITE (FROM LEFT): The ceiling at Garden of Delights is one of its many unique design highlights; mouth-watering cuisine awaits.

creative Peruvian ceviches and Latin American tapas. All of these are quite perfectly paired with exquisite bar specialities including mojitos, caipirinhas, pisco sour, chilled martinis, the splendid waft of Cuban cigars and what is probably one of the most impressive wine lists in the whole of Beijing—the latter encased in a glass show-cellar.

To keep the 'Beijing Latino' beat thumping, the Garden of Delights also puts on monthly culinary and wine promotions, wine and cigar dinners for special occasions and corporate events as well as offering special pre-concert cocktails and after concert dinners.

SEATS
80

FOOD
contemporary Latin American • ceviche and tapas • chocolate desserts

DRINK
extensive wine and cocktail list

FEATURES
Cuban cigars • live jazz

NEARBY
Forbidden City • Tiananmen Square

CONTACT
53 Donganmen Avenue Dongcheng District, Beijing 100006 • telephone: +86.10.5138 5688 • facsimile: +86.10.5138 5689 • email: info@gardenofdelights.com.cn • website: gardenofdelights.com.cn

jaan

...the glamour of 1920s China with the exquisite flavours of contemporary French cuisine...

Located within the exclusive domain of Raffles Beijing Hotel, Jaan combines the glamour of 1920s China with the exquisite flavours of contemporary French cuisine. Situated only minutes away from some of the city's most famed historic sights, including the Forbidden City, Tiananmen Square and the fast disappearing hutong alleys, the century-old hotel building housing Jaan has become an iconic landmark in Beijing's historical centre.

The hotel was opened in 1917 but recently closed for a year of renovations to revive the original features back to their former glory. Showcasing the vaulted ceilings and grand bay windows characteristic of the hotel's structure, Jaan offers guests a chance to eat, drink and embrace the surrounding architectural glory. Favoured by a host of literary and cultural luminaries including George Bernard Shaw, Henri Cartier-Bresson, Charles De Gaulle, Guo Moruo and Dr Sun Yat Sen, the original 1924 timber dance floor takes pride of place, on which the historic Bösendorfer piano grandly stands. Majestic French windows overlook Chang'an Avenue and dramatic chandeliers retain the sparkle of their 1920s heyday.

Seasonal appetisers include Pan-fried Foie Gras on Ratte Potato Purée with Winter Truffles, Marinated Mediterranean Tuna Belly and Scottish Salmon with a Tomato-Oyster Tartar; a salad of vegetables with orange marinade and carrot sorbet; and Lobster Carpaccio with Black Truffles, Spiced Tomato and Herb Salad. Soups, such as Jaan's Lobster Cappuccino with Sautéed Crab and Spring Onions, are served as a refresher course before moving on.

Guests can expect to enjoy dishes such as the Slow Oven-Roasted Brittany Cod with Lemon-Flavoured Champagne Sauce, Sole Fillet with a Ravioli of Fresh Oysters and Mussels, Grilled Maine Lobster with Fava Bean Fricassee and Vanilla Bouillon, Roast Venison with Grilled Chestnuts and a Grand Veneur sauce; Roasted Rack of Lamb with Crispy Potato and a Liquorice-Infused Natural Jus and Australian Wagyu Beef with Macaroni-Parmesan Gratin and Truffle Sauce. Jaan also hosts small- to medium-sized events with great success, and occasionally showcases the work of guest chefs.

Vegetarians are well catered for with choices including Asparagus and Morels in a Pink Garlic Cream and Porcini Risotto with Winter Truffles and Butternut Foam. There are also wines available from many of the best regions, and a reputation for some of the best value set menus in the city.

THIS PAGE (FROM TOP): *Expect only the very best French cuisine at Jaan at Raffles Beijing Hotel; a table at Jaan, exquisitely set with only the finest tableware; each dish is beautiful presented.*

OPPOSITE (FROM LEFT): *A private room offers more exclusivity; the frothy Lobster Cappuccino.*

SEATS
64

FOOD
modern French

DRINK
extensive wine list

FEATURES
colonial setting • open kitchen •
elegant design

NEARBY
Tiananmen Square • Silk Street
Market • Forbidden City

CONTACT
Raffles Beijing Hotel
33 East Chang'an Avenue
Dongcheng District, Beijing 100004 •
telephone: +86.10.6526 3388 •
facsimile: +86.10.8500 4380 •
email: beijing@raffles.com •
website: www.beijing.raffles.com

my humble house

...a palette of soothing pastels gives the restaurant a stylish edge...

Located above the Oriental Plaza, China's largest shopping complex, and adjacent to the Grand Hyatt Beijing, My Humble House is only a few minutes' walk from Beijing's most visited sights, including the Forbidden City and Tiananmen Square. Marking a significant milestone in the Tung Lok Group's 23-year history, the restaurant was opened in November 2004 following the success of My Humble House Singapore two years earlier.

The minimalism of renowned Japanese architect S Miura's design, based on a palette of soothing pastels, gives the restaurant a stylish edge and the modern Chinese cuisine easily stands up to the impressively stocked wine cellar. A long sleek bar, framed by the vast windows, allows guests to indulge in a cocktail (or two) before their meal.

Large tables are separated by split-levels and wide walkways. Private sections are available for advance bookings and are greatly in demand, while one exclusive private room even comes with its own fully stocked wine cellar, filled with a range of fine vintages from around the world. The polished blond wood floor of the entire dining area evokes a light, spacious feel while the glass roof lets natural light in by day and dramatically showcases the star-studded night sky in the evenings, adding to the delightful sense of openness.

The tableware at My Humble House is custom-made with unique shapes and designs. At one corner, an alcove has been transformed into a library which displays design and cookery books on glass shelves while a long table in the centre of the restaurant is perfect for larger parties and celebrations. Luxurious armchairs are upholstered in shades of cream and pale jade, with delicately embroidered cushions.

THIS PAGE (FROM TOP): One can look forward to innovative Chinese cuisine at My Humble House; its well-stocked wine cellar is a definite plus for connoisseurs.

OPPOSITE (CLOCKWISE FROM TOP): A choice dessert is the perfect end to a satisfying lunch or dinner; the restaurant is synonymous with style and sophistication; the massive glass roof forms an impressive canopy over diners.

The visual indulgences continue through to the domain of the kitchen where each dish is imaginatively sculpted to rarefied levels of presentation. For example, Steamed Glutinous Rice with Beef arrives artistically set in its leaf wrappings, while the exquisite shark's fin dish comes sealed in pastry which, when broken, reveals its highly prized maritime treasure.

At My Humble House, one finds all kinds of excellent seafood, including fresh prawns, lobster and the ultimate treat—abalone tuna.

SEATS
120

FOOD
modern Chinese

DRINK
extensive wine list • cocktails

FEATURES
bar • private dining rooms •
library • showpiece glass roof

NEARBY
Oriental Plaza • Temple of Heaven •
Forbidden City • Tiananmen Square

CONTACT
Beijing Oriental Plaza
Podium Level W3 #01-07
Office Towers, 1 East Chang'an Avenue
Dongcheng District, Beijing 100738 •
telephone: +86.10.8518 8811 •
facsimile: +86.10.8518 6249 •
email: mhh@tunglok.com •
website: www.tunglok.com

chang + biörck

...Scandinavian simplicity and functionality and rich Chinese detail.

THIS PAGE: A sample of products from Chang & Biörck, featuring the characteristic Scandinavian design aesthetic combined with Chinese patterns and materials.

OPPOSITE (CLOCKWISE FROM RIGHT): Chang & Biörck lamps light up any room in a range of colours; unique roll-up jewellery bags; Chang & Biörck's showroom.

Combining two of the world's most distinctive and recognised sets of design sensibilities—Scandinavian and Chinese—Chang & Biörck have created a fusion of both styles to produce a delightfully innovative and new-aesthetic range of home accessories.

The founders of the company, Eva Biörck and India Chang, are from Scandinavia and are now living in China. When they first set up the company, they invited a number of Scandinavian designers to come to China to experience the rich culture of the country and to gain an understanding of local manufacturing techniques and traditional designs. Since then, Scandinavian designers and Chinese craftsmen have collaborated to produce hand-made products using only the very highest quality Chinese materials such as silk, porcelain and gleaming lacquered wood. The results are spectacular—a fresh new perspective on home accessories with Scandinavian simplicity and functionality and rich Chinese detail.

Over the years, renowned designers specialising in textiles and porcelain have visited China with the aim of collaborating with Chang & Biörck, including Swedish designers Gunilla Lagerhem Ullberg and Marie-Louise Hellgren. One of Sweden's best-known textile designers, Ullberg has created a range of fabrics used in many of Chang & Biörck's products. Travel and nature are key elements in Gunilla's patterns and colour combinations. When creating fabrics for Chang & Biörck, she takes inspiration from traditional Chinese materials and marries these with Scandinavian designs, producing contemporary elegant fabrics. In 2003, Chang & Biörck received the Formidable prize at the Design Fair in Stockholm for her creation.

Hellgren works mainly with ceramics and functionality and elegance define her portfolio. Chang & Biörck feature her new bone china teapots as well as her mutually complementary teacups, Ao and Tu, which also stand as individual pieces. The saucers symbolise the sun and the moon, and were inspired by her visit to the altar at the Temple of Heaven in Beijing.

At Chang & Biörck, visitors can buy fabric by length or browse through products which include cushions, table runners, place mats, porcelain teapots and cups. Other creations at Chang & Biörck include beautiful Ming Dynasty-influenced table and floor lamps, with lacquered elm wood frame and lotus-style silk shade. Elm tea tables, with a latticed surface, can be used as flower stands or sofa tables. Other home accessories include jewellery rolls and boxes, cosmetic bags, slippers and ties.

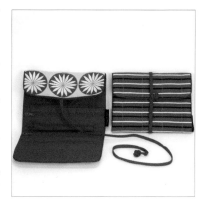

Chang & Biörck products are also available in various high-end lifestyle stores around the world. In China itself, customers can visit either Chang & Biörck's showroom near the Lama Temple in Beijing or at Marianne's Place in Shanghai.

PRODUCTS
tableware • lamps • fabrics • porcelain • cushions • tables

FEATURES
Scandinavian and Chinese designs

NEARBY
Lama Temple • Ghost Street

CONTACT
Sky & Sea Business Plaza, Building A Suite 511, 107 North Dongsi Avenue Dongcheng District, Beijing 100007 • telephone: +86 10 8400 2296 • email: info@changbiorck.com • website: www.changbiorck.com

shanghai tang

Renowned for combining traditional Chinese design and motifs with a contemporary edge...

THIS PAGE (FROM TOP): Bold colours characterise the design palette; each item is thoroughly modern, accented with traditional flavour.

OPPOSITE (CLOCKWISE FROM RIGHT): Glass windows offer a tantalising look into the shop and at its wares; home accessories are some of the best selling items available; shops are stylishly designed to showcase the products within.

Pre-liberation Shanghai was a hotbed of old-world glitz and glamour, synonymous with decadence at the very highest level of the city's 20th-century prominence. It was with this romantic era of style in mind that Shanghai Tang was created in 1994.

What first began as an imperial tailor shop soon grew into a worldwide business that can boast over 4 million visitors to its stores a mere six years later. Today, Shanghai Tang's chain of prestigious high-end boutiques offers a wide range of clothes for men, women and children, as well as chic home wares and accessories for the house-proud that bear the unmistakable stamp of the brand's signature witty Orient-meets-Occident design sensibilities.

Renowned for combining traditional Chinese design and motifs with a contemporary edge, resulting in what can only be termed a Nouveau Chinois style fusion, Shanghai Tang's creations are rich with opulent, bold colours such as vivid fuchsia and electrifying lime green. Attention to details, impeccable craftsmanship and an overall beautiful fit are all hallmarks of the brand's clothes, which have drawn a stellar fan base that includes everyone from Hollywood A-lister Whoopi Goldberg to Australian celebrity chef Kylie Kwong.

Season after season, Shanghai Tang dreams up designs that revitalise Chinese style by weaving it with the dynamism of the 21st century. One need look no further for an example of this than its 2007 Spring Summer collection, called Shanghai Modern. A nod to the new face of Shanghai, the collection features prints of the Pudong skyline with the iconic outline of the Oriental Pearl Tower. A more feminine counterpoint to the graphic and urban prints of Shanghai Modern is the Chinoiserie Over Lace collection. In this collection, birds and trees are delicately embroidered onto printed lace, creating a softer, timeless look evocative of the modern woman of all ages. Traditional cheongsam-style frocks with high, stiff collars are re-interpreted in silk georgette, chiffon and crêpe. A sneak peek at the Autumn Winter collection reveals an inspired line of luxe materials with design influences taken from the ancient Silk Road and its myriad of well-clothed merchants and traders from Mongolia to the fastnesses of Central Asia.

The Imperial Tailor service is still available to Shanghai Tang's most discerning customers, who can meet with a team of skilled craftsmen to customise a garment to their exact fit, with the option of adding any further personal specifications. All trimmings, piping and the intricate details are all hand-made and hand-sewn by the artisans, who also see to the construction of Shanghai Tang's signature oriental Chinese fastenings. A bespoke Shanghai Tang garment can take up to 10 days to complete, but the finished product, as customers attest, is worth the wait.

PRODUCTS
clothing • accessories • home ware

FEATURES
dynamic and vibrant designs

NEARBY
Forbidden City • Tiananmen Square •
Temple of Heaven • Great Wall

CONTACT
Grand Hyatt Beijing Shop 3 and 5
UG Level, 1 East Chang'an Avenue
Dongcheng District, Beijing 100738 •
telephone: +86.10.8518 0898 •
facsimile: +86.10.8518 2180

Beijing Capital International Airport
International Departure Lounge
Terminal 2, Beijing 100621 •
telephone: +86.10.6459 1356

email: contactus@shanghaitang.com •
website: www.shanghaitang.com

red gate gallery

...on the cutting edge of China's booming arts scene.

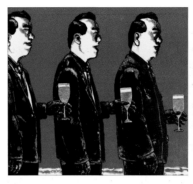

The year 2006 held a special significance for Red Gate Gallery as it celebrated its 15th anniversary and also opened a second outlet in the Beijing 798 Art Zone. Red Gate Gallery is the Chinese capital's oldest and most prominent contemporary art gallery.

Representing China's leading artists and emerging talents, Red Gate Gallery is on the cutting edge of China's booming arts scene. Of its two galleries which are owned by Australian Brian Wallace, the principal one is located in the Dongbianmen Watchtower. The watchtower, which is located directly east of the Tiananmen Square on the southeast corner of the old city wall, remains a precious monument of the old city as the only remaining Ming Dynasty corner tower. Visitors who climb the stairs to the battlements are treated to inspiring views across the city, and of the neighbouring Beijing Railway Station. The gallery has an exposed roof, slate floor, and huge red pillars bolstering vast beams. The contrast between old and new is strikingly apparent with huge contemporary artworks stretching across the ground floor and top mezzanine level.

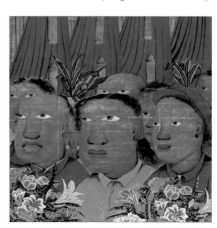

Located further out of town towards the airport, Red Gate's second gallery is in the Beijing 798 Art Zone which is home to Beijing's evolving art scene buzzing with galleries, artists and art

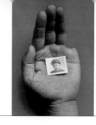

collectors. With tall, bright windows, white painted brick walls and a metal staircase leading to a viewing level, the gallery sets a very different tone from its historic, elder sibling.

The 19 artists represented by Red Gate Gallery express their awareness of China's rapidly changing society and observations of daily life through diverse media such as contemporary Chinese painting, collage, lithographs, oil paintings, photography and sculptures. They are concerned with issues such as economic change, gender, population, politics and the environment.

Past Red Gate Gallery exhibitions have featured painter, photographer and performance artist Sheng Qi who translated iconic images from the media onto large canvases. Renowned printmaker Zhou Jirong has showcased his work which portrayed the rapidly changing landscapes of Beijing in beautiful silkscreen prints. Other well-known Chinese artists represented include Su Xinping, Wang Yuping, Liu Qinghe, Zhu Wei and Li Gang.

Red Gate Gallery is also a major participant in the national and international arts community through two broad ranging residency programmes. One is for foreign artists, curators, writers and academics, while the other is an Artist in Residence programme targeted specifically at emerging Chinese artists from outside Beijing. This programme has proven to be very successful and resulted in many artists participating in exhibitions both in China and overseas. Red Gate Gallery is the only gallery in China offering such an opportunity to Chinese artists and this has enabled it to predict new trends and spot undiscovered talents.

PRODUCTS
oil paintings • sculptures • prints • photography • Chinese paintings

FEATURES
exhibitions and art fairs • wide selection

NEARBY
Ritan Park • Sanlitun

CONTACT
Dongbianmen Watchtower
Chongwen District, Beijing 100062 •
telephone: +86.10.6525 1005 •
facsimile: +86.10.6432 2624 •
email: redgategallery@aer.net.cn •
website: www.redgategallery.com

haidian

Qinghe Railway Station

Shangdi

Fifth Ring Road

Temple of the Reclining Buddha

Wofosi Road

Yiheyuan Road

Xiangshan Road

Yuquanshan Road

Summer Palace

Kunming Lake

grant Hills Park (Xiangshan)

South Xiangshan Road

Kunminghu Road

Old Summer Palace

West Qinghua Road

North Zhongguancun Avenue

Peking University

Tsinghua University

Wudaokou

Northwest Fourth Ring Road

Hailong Shopping Mall

Zhongguancun Avenue

Qinghuayuan Railway Station

Zhichunlu

Dazhongsi

Chang River

Northwest Third Ring Road

Wanshou Temple + Beijing Art Museum

South Zhongguancun Avenue

Gaoliangqiao Bending Road

Jishuitan

Zizhuyuan Road

Beijing Aquarium

Beijing North Railway Station

Xizhimen

Xihuangcun Railway Station

Wulu Railway Station

Purple Bamboo Garden

Beijing Zoo

Xizhimen Avenue

Beijing Exhibition Hall

Beijing Planetarium

Xizhimen

N

> The Shangri-La Hotel, Beijing
> CHI, The Spa

Diaoyutai State Guest House

Yuyuan Lake

Guchenglu   Bajiao Youleyuan   Yuquanlu   Wanshoulu   Junshibowuguan   Muxidi

Babaoshan   Wukesong   Gongzhufen

Legend

	Expressway
	Urban ring road
	Main road
	Other road
	Railway
	Railway station
	Light rail
	Subway
○	Subway/light rail station
◎	Water

0 km   0.5   1   1.5   2 km

heralding the future

Haidian is the university quarter and is home to some of the leading universities in the country, including Peking University and Tsinghua University. Respectively known as the Harvard and MIT of China, both date back more than 100 years and count the nation's most prominent movers and shakers among their graduates. This bustling area also contains China's Silicon Valley, with many high-tech companies set up here, such as Microsoft, Lenovo, Siemens, Huawei, NEC, and Sun Microsystems, just to name a few.

The high-tech boom—which has resulted in an explosion of tech-savvy companies in Haidian—and the universities' scrambling to accommodate their rapidly increasing student intakes have undoubtedly changed the face of this once-sleepy area. At the same time, companies and research facilities are taking advantage of the synergy between each other to grow even faster.

Despite this, and despite being to the far northwest of the old imperial capital, the area is also rich in old temples and sprawling parks.

This is a great place to mix with China's increasingly ambitious university students. In many ways, Chinese students today live similarly to their counterparts in the West. The streets around the schools are lined with bookstores, coffee shops, bars, clothing stores, and small eateries. Bookstore shelves are piled high with Western works, in translation and in the original language, including Simone de Beauvoir's biography, Orwell's *1984*, the bestseller *The Da Vinci Code*, and Francis Bacon's *Essays*.

One summer morning, just inside the main gate of Peking University, two students kiss beneath a tree. A few yards away, students lie on the grass beside a small lake, reading textbooks or just chatting. Meanwhile, a male Chinese student with dyed blond hair and a gold earring, and wearing a T-shirt that says 'Che Guevara', paces back and forth while memorising from a textbook.

THIS PAGE (FROM TOP): *Early evening at the bustling Wudaokou junction in Haidian district; memorial gate at the leading Tsinghua University, widely regarded as the MIT of China.*

OPPOSITE: *Entrance to Beijing's prestigious Peking University.*

PAGE 164: *Large, colourful balloons depicting Peking opera masks float over Kunming Lake in the Summer Palace.*

electronic paradise

Many visitors to China think this is the place to get that good deal on a digital camera or computer, but they are most likely confusing mainland China with nearby Hong Kong, where even the prices there are still probably slightly higher than in the United States. Imported high-end electronics are usually slapped with a high import tax, often making them considerably more expensive here than back at home. In any case, they're never cheaper, and you often find older models on the store shelves. The exception is mobile phones, which is a booming business here in China, with some people trading in their 'old' models for new ones every six months.

But if you're looking for no-frills, high-tech gadgets, this is the place to shop. The spacious five-storey Hailong Shopping Mall in Zhongguancun, also known as China's Silicon Valley, is a one-stop shopping destination for cheap electronics: locally slapped-together computers, MP3 players, backup drives, wireless cards, memory chips and many other components. But buyer beware—the quality is often uneven here.

nightlife

Wudaokou has a bustling night scene reminiscent of college towns everywhere. Dine at one of the many international restaurants—Korean, Mexican, Japanese, Italian, American, or just about anything else you could want—before heading out for a night on the town. Or kill two birds with one stone at the very popular Lush, opposite the Wudaokou Light Rail Station. A favourite of both foreign and Chinese students, Lush has a decent Western menu and a well-stocked bar, and organises special events in the evenings: Latin nights, live music, and salsa classes. Sunday is open mic night.

If dancing is your thing, head to the basement of Propaganda, which is packed with Korean and Western students, especially on Wednesdays—open bar night. Get

THIS PAGE (FROM TOP): A modern sculpture graces the front of the sleek Tsinghua Science Park; excited students moshing at the Midi Music Festival, held annually in Haidian.
OPPOSITE: A night scene lit by brilliant neon lights in the busy Wudaokou student district.

there early because it can be close to impossible to squeeze past T-shirted students to get a drink at the bar. For something a tad more sophisticated, and to escape from all those young students, check out the trendy Zub, a basement bar-cum-club serving upmarket cocktails and featuring music spun by local deejays.

For those serious about their music, a visit to D-22 is a must on the itinerary. This bar-club is dedicated to identifying and supporting talented young musicians and artists in Beijing, and boasts one of the best live music sound systems in China. The club also invites leading experimental musicians from the United States, Japan, Europe and elsewhere to perform here and collaborate with local musicians.

fragrant hills park

While Haidian, with its frenzied activity and vibrant nightlife, is the city's university and high-tech centre, a good deal of Old Beijing still remains here, much of it calm in comparison to the rest of the district. The pleasant and sprawling Fragrant Hills Park first emerged in 1168 during the Jin Dynasty (1115–1234), but like many historical sites, it underwent numerous reconstructions and expansions, most notably in the Yuan, Ming

and Qing Dynasties. Fragrant Hills has more than two dozen pools, pavilions, temples and ancient trees, and a number of old structures that were damaged by invading Western troops during the final decades of the Qing Dynasty.

On a slope in the park stands the Temple of the Azure Clouds—best known for its Indian-influenced Varja Throne Pagoda, and a hall housing 500 life-sized wooden and gilt arhat (one who has reached enlightenment). Once the home of a Yuan Dynasty general, it was converted into a Buddhist temple in 1366, and expanded again in the 16th and 17th centuries by imperial eunuchs who wished to be buried here. The temple was damaged during the Cultural Revolution (1966–76) but has since been nicely restored.

temple of the reclining buddha

The Temple of the Reclining Buddha was built in the Tang Dynasty and rebuilt and renamed several times through the years. The Hall of the Sleeping Buddha—the main building in this temple complex—is most famous for its large, bronze statue of Sakyamuni Buddha in a recumbent position. Cast in 1321, the statue weighs a hefty 54 tonnes and stands more than 5 m (16 ft) tall. Surrounding it are 12 clay disciples, who are thought to be listening to the Buddha's final instructions before the end of his earthly life.

summer retreats

In Haidian, one can retreat from Beijing's intense summer heat and enjoy the lazy lakes and pavilions of the Summer Palace, known in Chinese as Yiheyuan. Once reserved solely for royalty, the large park was created by the first emperor of the Jin Dynasty, and enhanced by following dynasties. During the Second Opium War in 1860, British and French soldiers fighting in China damaged the park; mere decades later, the park was again razed by foreign soldiers who were lifting the siege against the foreign Legation Quarter during the Boxer Rebellion of 1900.

With beautiful, sprawling gardens and complexes romantically named Hall of Dispelling Clouds, Floating Heart Bridge, and Gate of Welcoming the Moon, the Summer Palace is a perfect place for a leisurely stroll. From Longevity Hill—on which the Jin emperor constructed his Gold Mountain Palace—visitors can also enjoy vistas across Kunming Lake. A 700-m (2,297-ft) Long Corridor, a covered walkway, runs along the north shore of the lake, and is decorated with auspicious symbols and paintings. The Hall of Jade

Ripples is where the notorious Cixi locked away the young Emperor Guangxu in 1898 after he tried to implement far-reaching changes in the Hundred Days' Reform Movement. He was to remain a prisoner here until he passed away suddenly in 1908. There are rumours that he was poisoned by Cixi, who died one day later. A famous marble boat is docked at the west end of the lake; it was built by Cixi with money allegedly intended to create a modern Chinese navy.

The nearby Old Summer Palace, or Yuanmingyuan, is a complex of three large gardens, designed for Emperor Qianlong by Jesuit architects who served in his Qing Dynasty court. Like Yiheyuan, the site also suffered damage by invading foreign troops in 1860 and 1900, and little remains of it today aside from some ruins.

THIS PAGE (FROM TOP): A red temple door rimmed by yellow and green glazed Buddhas at the Pagoda of Buddhist Virtue; a Buddhist tower on a hillside overlooking Kunming Lake.
OPPOSITE: A vast field of wild flowers at the Summer Palace.

wanshou temple

The Wanshou Temple—also known as the mini Forbidden City—dates back to 1577, when it was built by a wealthy eunuch, who was soon to fall from grace due to court intrigues that wracked the final years of the Ming Dynasty. The structure is one of many that were restored by Emperor Qianlong. This temple was a place for the imperial family to celebrate birthdays, and also to rest and change boats when making their retreat to the Summer Palace. The Beijing Art Museum, located on the grounds of the temple, features a significant collection of ancient bronzes, jade, pottery, porcelain, paintings and many more national treasures.

...the Summer Place is a perfect place for a leisurely stroll.

the shangri-la hotel, beijing

...a prime location near Beijing's bustling business district...

THIS PAGE (FROM LEFT): *Elements of fengshui incorporated in the design of the hotel lobby; travellers can expect nothing but comfort and luxury at the Shangri-La Hotel, Beijing.*

OPPOSITE (CLOCKWISE FROM LEFT): *Enjoy cocktails at the Cloud Nine Bar; a traditional Tibetan singing bowl used at CHI, The Spa; visitors can enjoy the great outdoors in the hotel's garden; a lavish selection of delicacies at Café Cha's seafood station.*

With a prime location near Beijing's bustling business district, Shangri-La Hotel, Beijing is immensely popular with vacationers and business travellers alike. Listed on *Condé Nast Traveller*'s 2003 Gold List, it was also voted the 'Best Hotel in Beijing' by *Global Finance* in 2004 and one of the 'Top 3 Business Hotels in Beijing' by *Asiamoney* in 2006.

In March 2007, Shangri-La Hotel, Beijing completed its US$50 million expansion project, bringing its number of guestrooms to 670 with the unveiling of the new sophisticated Valley Wing located in a 17-storey modern glass tower. With a walk-in wardrobe and a spacious lounge area, each premier room in the Valley Wing measures at least 50 sq m (538 sq ft) and features high-speed and wireless Internet access. Complimentary breakfast and beverages, including champagne, wines and canapés, are available all day in the grand Valley Wing Lounge, the largest executive lounge among Shangri-La Hotels and Resorts worldwide.

CHI, The Spa, is also a brand-new facility at the hotel covering 1,000 sq m (10,764 sq ft) and is equipped with 11 luxurious private suites. The exclusive treatment rooms are modern interpretations of a Tibetan temple with Himalayan art and decorations. The combination of

scented incense, music from Tibetan singing bowls, and shimmering light contributes to a serene atmosphere. At the health club, one is spoilt for choice with the wide variety of fitness facilities such as the 25-m (82-ft) heated indoor pool, whirlpool, sauna, steam room and an outdoor jogging track on the rooftop garden.

Visitors can also take an hour-long cruise on the River Dragon, an 11-m- (36-ft-) long vessel commissioned exclusively by Shangri-La Hotel, Beijing. The 38-seat traditionally designed barge heads towards the Summer Palace along the Chang River and recreates the imperial route that only members of the Chinese royalty enjoyed in the past. The ride offers views of ancient bridges, temples and courtyard houses on the riverbanks and ends with a fully guided tour at the historical Summer Palace.

The addition of Blu Lobster, a contemporary restaurant and cocktail lounge, enhances the dining experience with its inventive Western cuisine and one of the finest selection of Bordeaux wines in Beijing. Other restaurants include Shang Palace which focuses on Cantonese specialities, Café Cha with its open kitchens and individual food stations, and Nishimura which has a sushi bar, teppanyaki, robatayaki and traditional tatami rooms. Visitors can also enjoy cocktails at Cloud Nine Bar, voted the 'Best Hotel Bar in Beijing' by *Forbes* in 2005.

ROOMS
670

FOOD
Blu Lobster: Western • Nishimura: Japanese • Shang Palace: Cantonese • Café Cha: international • The Garden Bar and Terrace: snacks

DRINK
Cloud Nine Bar • Lobby Lounge

FEATURES
health club • indoor pool • spa • business centre • cigar shop • shopping arcade • limousine service

NEARBY
Summer Palace • Beijing Zoo • Yuyuan Lake • Beijing Exhibition Hall • Beijing Art Museum • Yuetan Park • Beijing Planetarium

CONTACT
29 Zizhuyuan Road Haidian District, Beijing 100089 • telephone: +86.10.6841 2211 • facsimile: +86.10.6841 8002/3 • email: slb@shangri-la.com • website: www.shangri-la.com

chi, the spa

...the exotic Himalayas combined with ancient Chinese healing traditions and rituals.

In traditional Chinese philosophy, 'qi', otherwise known as 'chi', is the universal life force that fundamentally drives our well-being and vitality, energising and sustaining us all. It is believed that chi must be able to flow freely within the body in order to maintain good health. Such are the beliefs and, subsequently, the practices maintained behind Shangri-La Hotel Beijing's much-anticipated and newly opened wellness facility, CHI, The Spa.

Drawing its inspiration from Shangri-La, the mythical utopian valley holding the secrets to eternal youth and life, CHI, The Spa's treatments reflect the magical world of the exotic Himalayas combined with ancient Chinese healing traditions and rituals. These therapies, carefully developed by a dedicated team of wellness experts, are based on the five elements in Chinese philosophy of metal, water, wood, fire and earth to harmonise the body's yin and yang energies and restore a natural balance of health.

Upon arrival at the spa reception, clad in rich shades of dark wood and natural fabrics, guests are given a personal consultation with a trained spa professional to determine their five-element readings, unique to each individual, ensuring that all guests experience only treatments that are the most suited to their needs.

In Chi Balance, a blend of Asian techniques is individually tailored for each guest's yin and yang status. Focusing on the three elements of earth, wood and fire, these techniques include acupressure, an energising, rejuvenating massage for yang stimulation, and a relaxing, calming massage for yin tranquillity. In the Aroma Vitality treatment, the massage is a gentler combination, with elements of Swedish, shiatsu and reflexology, combined with the therapeutic qualities of Oriental aromatic essential oils.

In the meantime, other CHI, The Spa therapies like the Himalayan Healing Stone Massage and the Mountain Tsampa Rub make full use of indigenous ingredients and techniques drawn from ancient folk healing traditions of the Himalayan mountains and its surrounding regions. Other signature treatments at CHI which will catch the eyes of spa visitors include Enchanted Journey and the Vitality Ritual, which can last up to a total of five exquisite hours of one-on-one

THIS PAGE (FROM TOP): CHI, The Spa's signature aromatherapy treatments perfume the air; the herbal pound is only one example of the traditional folk remedies available at the spa.

OPPOSITE (FROM TOP): Fragrant wafts of burning incense imbue the atmosphere with an exotic feel; a luxurious spa treatment room; complete relaxation awaits spa visitors at this restful sanctuary.

ROOMS
11 treatment suites

FEATURES
private bathing, changing, shower and herbal steam facilities • retail gallery • hydrotherapy suite spa • nail lounge • unique Burmese and Tibetan antiques and artworks

NEARBY
Diaoyutai State Guest House • Beijing Exhibition Hall • Beijing Zoo • Beijing Ocean Aquarium • Purple Bamboo Garden • Summer Palace

CONTACT
The Shangri-La Hotel, Beijing
29 Zizhuyuan Road
Haidian District, Beijing 100089 •
telephone: +86.10.6841 2211 •
facsimile: +86.10.6841 8002/3 •
website: www.shangri-la.com

pampering and indulgence by fully-trained spa professionals. The Vitality Ritual is a half-day experience, popular with Beijing's well-heeled high society doyennes, that thoroughly and methodically revitalises the whole body, encompassing Uplifting Himalayan Bath Therapy, Revitalising Essential Wrap, Mountain Tsampa Rub and Himalayan Healing Stone Massage.

All these can be experienced in any one of CHI, The Spa's 11 luxurious private treatment suites—known to be some of the largest in Beijing—that have been designed and styled as a modern interpretation of a Tibetan lamasery with Himalayan-inspired art and accessories. To add to the mystical aura of the legend of the hidden sanctuary Shangri-La are the soothing sounds of Tibetan singing bowls in the background, moving shafts of warm, soft lighting and the exotically sweet scent of burning incense wafting through the air.

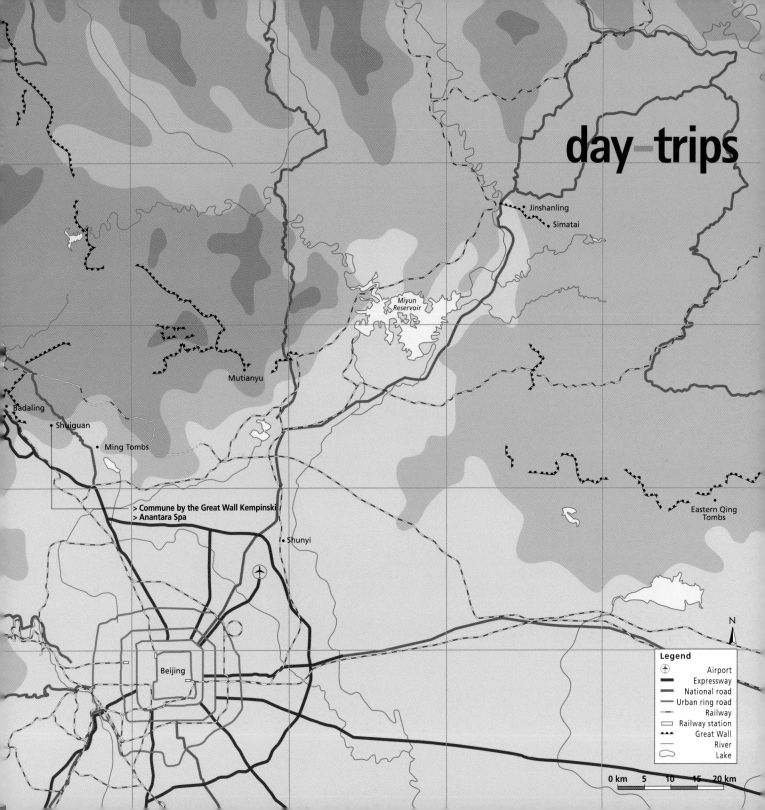

day-trips

Jinshanling
Simatai

Miyun
Reservoir

Mutianyu

Badaling
Shuiguan
Ming Tombs

Eastern Qing
Tombs

> Commune by the Great Wall Kempinski
> Anantara Spa

Shunyi

Beijing

N

0 km   5   10   15   20 km

off the beaten path

The northern fringes of Beijing were primarily farm fields just two decades ago. Today, this is the site of many of Beijing's fanciest villas, and the home of well-heeled expatriates and Chinese entrepreneurs. This area also includes great outdoor sites: the Great Wall, the Ming and Qing Dynasty imperial tombs, and many hiking areas. Besides the easily accessible Badaling and Mutianyu, which have undergone extensive renovation, parts of the wall—such as Jinshanling and Simatai—remain relatively untouched.

shunyi

Jingshun (Beijing-Shunyi) Road is a four-lane highway crowded with exhaust-spewing automobiles and dodging bicyclists and pedestrians weaving in and out of traffic. The sides of this chaotic thoroughfare are graced with a different image, however: huge billboards gushing about marvellous new villas, many with boastful claims and artistic renditions exaggerating the landscaping of these complexes.

This once-sleepy farm area is now home to foreign and Chinese high rollers, who have snapped up the luxury villas dotting the area. American-themed residential communities—with names like Chateau Regalia, Capital Paradise, Eurovillage, Beijing Riviera, La Leman Lake, Gahood Villas, and Villa Yosemite—are popping up all over Shunyi, luring American and European expatriates wishing to recreate their Western lifestyles, or wealthy Chinese seeking the comfort of a pseudo-American lifestyle. The going price for a 557-sq-m (6,000-sq-ft) home is more than RMB5.3 million (US$700,000), this in a city where annual per capita income stood at RMB15,600 (US$2,062) in 2006. That's a lot of gold dust for most Beijingers, but sales appear to be booming.

Residents of these communities—just 24 km (15 miles) from the Central Business District—live in two- and three-storey cookie cutter homes with large backyards for barbecuing, and community swimming pools and tennis courts built around clubhouses.

THIS PAGE: Security guards walk ahead of the crowd during a rehearsal for the first pop music festival on the Great Wall.

OPPOSITE: A distant tower seen through a battlement along the Jinshanling section of the wall.

PAGE 178: On the outskirts of Beijing, by the Great Wall, a man walks precariously along the rim of a large dam.

Close by, the RMB530 million (US$70 million) International School of Beijing is furnished with state-of-the-art facilities. Over at Pinnacle Plaza, one finds Subway, Starbucks, Domino's Pizza, a vet with barking dogs and meowing cats in cages out front, and Jenny Lou's, a busy grocery store stocked with American imports: Gatorade, Frosted Flakes, Pop Tarts, Aunty Jemima Pancake Syrup, and bottled Starbucks Mocha Frappucino.

Shunyi is also one of the key sites for the 2008 Olympics, and new highways are being laid down to conveniently move spectators to and from the area—some 36 km (22 miles) away from downtown Beijing—and to cut travel time in half to 30 minutes. The state-of-the-art Shunyi Olympic Rowing-Canoeing Park is being built in the district and will be the third largest arena for athletes vying for as many as 32 gold medals, including marathon swimming, rowing, canoeing and kayaking. The builders claim this

THIS PAGE: A construction worker walking along the site of the Olympic Rowing-Canoeing Park in northeastern Beijing.

OPPOSITE: (FROM TOP): Helicopter used in the protection of the Great Wall, sections of which are rapidly disappearing; kayakers coast along the surface of a Beijing lake.

is the most advanced venue in the world for rowing and canoeing, and that it is the first to have both a flat-water area and a competition course for slalom. As with many other Olympic venues, the Rowing-Canoeing Park is being built with the purpose of turning it over to public use at the end of the Olympics. After the Games, the park will be used for competitions, training, recreation and fitness, and looks set to become the largest holiday resort in northeastern Beijing.

But Shunyi is not just about villas and Olympics. The district today delivers some 8 million ducks each year to Beijing's roast duck restaurants. It's also home to the Yanjing Brewery (Yanjing is the old name of Beijing) and the Erguotou distillery, which produces baijiu, Beijing's famous grain-distilled white spirit.

shuiguan

Shuiguan (Water Pass) was built in the Ming Dynasty (1368–1644), as part of the defence system of the Badaling Great Wall. The area's main defence, however, was not bricks, but the force of torrential water flowing between the two mountains. This is one of the best-preserved parts of the Great Wall, snaking its way across the countryside for about 1 km (0.6 miles), with eight towers poking their heads up into the sky. Standing in the arrow tower, one can easily conjure up vivid scenes of ancient battles, as soldiers stared down apprehensively at fierce invaders approaching from the north.

Shuiguan is home to the Commune by the Great Wall Kempinski, a collection of 11 modern villas and a clubhouse, each designed by one of 12 well-known Asian architects, and each with a partial view of the Great Wall. This contemporary hotel-cum-living museum managed by the Kempinski Hotel aims to spur an appreciation of modern Asian architecture and to provide a quiet, swank retreat from the hustle and bustle of the city. The complex has several special trails leading to wild sections of the Great Wall, and will be duplicated in new phases in an adjacent area.

the great wall

Contrary to popular myth, the Great Wall was never actually a single wall, but many walls snaking along a 6,400-km (4,000-mile) east-west path across northern China. Some of these barricades are said to date as far back as 7 BCE, but most of what we think of today as the Great Wall was built, renovated or fortified during the Ming Dynasty. There is another popular belief that the Great Wall is a long defensive line

built by countless slaves working under the orders of Emperor Qin Shi Huang, who reigned from 259 to 210 BCE, and that he connected the smaller defensive walls of earlier states into a unified structure. However, the history of the Great Wall is far more complicated than this. As scholars have shown, the walls of rammed earth constructed under the first emperor of the Qin Dynasty were a far cry from the imposing Ming Dynasty stone walls that we ascend today in the area to the north of Beijing.

ABOVE: *The Great Wall rises and falls along with the contour of the terrain at Mutianyu, a popular site with tourists, which has undergone much reconstruction in recent years. Offering traditional views of the wall, this section shows a guardhouse in the distance.*

badaling and mutianyu

Just a little over an hour from Beijing, these two accessible parts of the Great Wall are popular among tourists with limited time on their hands. The one problem is that they're also crowded with hawkers, T-shirt sellers, souvenir stalls, fast-food joints and camel-riding photo opportunities. While the sites afford postcard views of the wall and surrounding countryside, when you get up close, you'll see that these sections were perhaps restored with too heavy a hand.

jinshanling and simatai

The Jinshanling and Simatai sections of the Great Wall rest on the steep slopes of Miyun county, to the north of Beijing. These have been less tinkered with and are favourite destinations for Beijing residents, who do the rugged four-hour walk from one end to the other.

Simatai, which has more beacon towers than other parts of the wall, was a priority restoration project in 2004 by officials who had learnt from past restoration efforts that had done more damage than good. Using traditional materials and technologies, these skilled workers reconstructed partially collapsed gates, battlements and sections of the wall.

Imperial history still emanates from the crumbling bricks, tangled undergrowth and natural settings of these damaged but grand sites. The worrying question is how much longer they can survive.

THIS PAGE: A group of tourists prepares to take the easy way down from the Great Wall at Badaling via a sled. At Mutianyu, one can likewise be whisked to the top of the wall on a cable car, and then slide back down on a 'toboggan'.

OPPOSITE: Conical straw farmers' hats hang from a line at a hawker's stall along the wall.

cultural revolution?

Since Manchu troops flooded south through an opening in the Great Wall at Shanhaiguan in 1644, obviating the need for a defence barrier to keep out 'northern barbarians', natural and man-made forces have worked hand in hand to slowly eat away at remaining parts of the wall. Today, the Great Wall of China is by turns crumbling, Disney-fied, and peppered with new gaps that you could literally drive a truck through. According to a survey of 100 sections of the wall carried out by the Great Wall Society of China, 30 per cent of the Great Wall is in ruins, and another 20 per cent is in 'reasonable' condition. The remaining 50 per cent has disappeared.

For his new book, *The Great Wall Revisited*, William Lindesay gathered hundreds of old photos of the Great Wall. He then set out to re-photograph 150 of the locations in the earlier images, creating sobering pairs of then-and-now scenes. In some cases, he found that sections had disappeared altogether. 'The Great Wall's greatness lies in its totality,' says Lindesay. 'If there's one brick less, or another gap to make way for a dirt road, then the continuity of the wall is broken and the value is reduced.'

Some of the greatest destruction has been fairly recent. In the 1950s, for example, Chinese leader Mao Zedong exhorted the masses to 'jingui, jinyong', or 'allow the past to serve the present'. Farmers were thus encouraged to demolish parts of the wall and use the bricks for building houses, pigpens, and walls.

As capitalism began making inroads in the 1980s, many officials believed that tourism bucks would save the wall. But today, the industry poses the biggest threat to the wall's survival. Poorly executed restoration efforts have left sections near the capital looking like a Hollywood set. Meanwhile, entrepreneurs have set up cable cars, souvenir stalls, fast-food restaurants, amusement facilities, villas, and crowded parking lots—all within a stone's throw of the structure.

The wall's biggest problem today is perhaps the lack of understanding among the Chinese, many of whom do not seem to realise the true significance of the Great Wall. The survey team, for instance, found parts of the wall covered in Chinese graffiti, and

farmers carting bricks away from the wall, just as they've been doing for decades. Three men in Inner Mongolia were detained for taking earth from a 2,200-year-old section of the wall to use as a landfill for a village factory. 'It's just a pile of earth,' village head Hao Zengjun told the official Xinhua News Agency.

Fortunately, a new national law was drafted in 2006 that aims to protect the national treasure. It is now illegal to remove bricks or stones from the wall, carve names in the bricks, hold raves on the wall, or build a house against the wall. Also important, the law says that 'all citizens, legal entities and organisations' are charged with protecting the wall and reporting illegal activity to government agencies.

However, the first penalties have been relatively mild and only time will tell if this is going to have an impact. On December 3, 2006, a construction company became the first to be fined under the new rules. For dismantling large pieces of the wall to make way for an illegal highway, the builders were fined the equivalent of US$6,500.

imperial tombs

A valley just 59 km (31 miles) north of Beijing, on the way to Badaling, was chosen in 1409 as the final resting place for the Ming Dynasty emperors. Taking into account traditional precepts of Chinese fengshui, or geomancy, the 13 tombs (three other emperors were buried elsewhere) are scattered over a basin approximately 40 sq km (15 sq miles), surrounded by mountains on three sides and facing the Beijing Plain in the south. Emperor Chongzhen, who hung himself in April 1644 as rebels crashed the gates of the imperial city, was the last Ming emperor to be buried here. The Manchu successors to the throne gave him a fitting burial in line with Chinese imperial protocol, albeit on a smaller scale than his predecessors.

The Eastern Qing Tombs, 125 km (78 miles) northeast of the capital, and a two-hour or longer drive away, are said to be more extravagant and interesting—and in better condition—than their Ming cousins. The site holds the remains of five emperors, 15 empresses and 136 royal concubines. It was chosen by Emperor Shunzhi, the first Qing emperor to rule over China, who stumbled upon the site while on a hunting trip. Of the nine tombs open to visitors, two are particularly noteworthy: that of Emperor Qianlong, who died in 1799, and Empress Dowager Cixi, who died in 1908.

Kuomintang General Sun Dianying and his army carried out a methodical looting of the complex in 1928, stripping it of Cixi's precious ornaments. The complex was restored by the People's Republic of China, and it is still today one of the most elaborate of the Eastern Qing tombs and the most splendid architecturally. A side hall displays some of the personal effects Cixi had amassed over the years. An enormous stone tablet takes up the entire middle section of the steps leading to the main hall of the mausoleum. Its high relief is adorned at the top with a phoenix (a symbol of the empress) and at the bottom, a dragon (a symbol of the emperor), suggesting that the Empress Dowager was of far greater importance than the emperors—which was indeed the case for much of her life in the imperial court.

THIS PAGE: *The Hall of Eminent Favour at Changling, the tomb of Ming Emperor Yongle, the 'architect of Beijing'.*

OPPOSITE: *The body of the dead emperor was carried down the Spirit Way, a 7-km (4-mile) path lined with large, carved stone animals—mythical and real—and imperial officials that ran from the Memorial Arch to the gate of the main tomb.*

...the final resting place for the Ming Dynasty emperors...

commune by the great wall kempinski

...a remarkable private collection of contemporary architecture.

THIS PAGE (FROM TOP): *Full-height windows give an unobstructed view of the surrounding area; the magnificent landscape as seen from an open-air terrace; children will find much to like.*

OPPOSITE (CLOCKWISE FROM TOP): *Young guests are kept happy and busy; bamboo slats create a tranquil place of light and artful shadow; sleek interiors soothe the senses; an airy space with bright walls.*

Set in 8 sq km (3 sq miles) of private land in the Badaling Mountains, near the Shuiguan section of the Great Wall, Commune by the Great Wall Kempinski is a remarkable private collection of contemporary architecture. Designed by 12 renowned Asian architects, 46 exclusive villas are dramatically studded across the steep slope of the valley offering remarkable views of the Great Wall and the awe-inspiring mountain landscape.

Only an hour from central Beijing, and a mere 40 minutes from the airport, the Commune guarantees a unique rural experience, a luxurious destination for a romantic getaway, holiday with family or friends, a private party or corporate event. Originally comprising of 11 villas and President Suites, ranging in size from 300 to 700 sq m (3,230 to 7,530 sq ft), individually designed by architects from across Asia, the Commune has recently opened an additional 31 villas based on the four most popular of its designs. Created by Gary Chang, the Suitcase House exhibits a humorous yet practical approach to modern design. Having entered the main chamber, guests might need a little help in finding their way around. The bedroom, bathroom,

kitchen and sauna are beneath floor hatches, leaving an open living space unhindered by conventions of interior design. The roof terrace is accessed via a pull-down staircase. With four bedrooms, a glass-encased sitting room and a sleek kitchen, the Bamboo House is a semi-rustic structure inspired by the geometries of bamboo scaffolding. The bamboo slats cast shadows across the slate floor and water features throughout the building. The newly opened villas in the Stone Valley are rented out by the room while President suites in the Walnut Valley can be only booked by the whole, catering to larger groups.

With satellite cable channels, DVD players, broadband Internet access, hi-fi systems and 24-hour butler service, guests can monitor the pulse of everyday life. Being surrounded by the peace and beauty of rural China, however, many visitors may decide to focus on more back-to-basic and relaxing pursuits. Shuiguan Great Wall & Badaling Great Wall are only a few minutes' drive from the Commune—a private experience of one of China's most famed and historical sights. Private roof terraces, balconies and lawns with dramatic views of the Great Wall offer picturesque settings for reading and resting. The Club House includes a library, lounge, a function hall and a pool, while its restaurants serve Chinese and Western cuisine using a wide range of locally grown organic ingredients. In addition, 24 Café in the stone village serves western food and Anantara Spa offers 15 treatment suites overlooking the mountainous backdrop.

ROOMS:
201

FOOD:
Courtyard Restaurant: Chinese

DRINK:
Wine Bar • Gallery's Lounge • Terrace

FEATURES:
movie theatre • pool • Anantara Spa • Kid's Club • helipad • 24-hour butler service • high-speed Internet access

NEARBY:
Great Wall • Ming Tombs • ski resorts • golf courses • vineyard

CONTACT:
The Great Wall Exit at Shuiguan, Badaling Highway, Beijing 100022 • telephone: +86.10.8118 1888 • facsimile: +86.10.8118 1866 • email: reservation@commune.com.cn • website: www.commune.com.cn

anantara spa

Anantara Spa offers visitors peace and tranquillity...

Located an hour's drive from Beijing, Anantara Spa offers visitors peace and tranquillity at Commune By the Great Wall Kempinski. The spa is designed on three levels and covers 1,000 sq m (10,800 sq ft), set against the awe-inspiring backdrop of the Badaling Mountains and the Great Wall. Villas are located on the slopes of the mountain range, and the entire Commune Resort is an architectural and design showpiece created by various renowned architects hailing from locations around Asia.

Anantara Spa, which opened in September 2006, is MSPA International's fourth spa in China. MSPA further operates spas throughout Asia, the Middle East and Africa and has put its vast experience in the wellness industry to full use in Anantara Spa by the Great Wall.

Guests of Anantara Spa experience an environment of serene contemplation, combining modern architecture and ancient surroundings. A total of 15 single or couple spa suites, designed to provide privacy and space for all guests, feature steam showers, wooden bath tubs and ample relaxation and changing areas. The spa is completed by a full-service beauty salon and a Yoga Deck, where classes are conducted with magnificent views of the Great Wall.

Anantara Spa experiences draw on the richness of the surrounding cultures as well as the philosophy of 'flow of water without borders'. Guests may choose from the spa's signature journey and rituals or create their own individual experience. Treatments draw from

Ayurveda, Balinese, Thai and Chinese techniques. Fresh indigenous ingredients are used throughout, such as ylang ylang, lemongrass, ginger, local fruits, natural volcanic pumice, powdered spices, organic honey, yoghurt and cucumber.

In the signature treatment, 'Culture of Anantara,' a Floral Foot Bath leads into a Sandalwood and Ginger Oriental Massage, followed by a nourishing Walnut, Green Tea and Honey Body Polish, and the journey into wellness is completed by an Aromatic Flower Bath.

For those who wish to indulge in a full-day Anantara Spa journey, the 'Anantara Rejuvenation' includes Ayurvedic Steam, Rose Body Polish, Honey and Milk Bath, Aromatherapy Massage, Rejuvenating Facial and choice of Manicure or Pedicure. Spa cuisine and refreshments are served during this total treatment immersion. Men are invited to enjoy spa treatments such as the 'Gentleman's Own Facial' or the 'Mountain Retreat.'

Shrouded in legacies and folktales of times past, each Anantara Spa can be found nestled in settings that interweave nature with tradition, and is designed to stir the movements of human emotion. If balance, energy and a sense of peace and tranquillity are qualities that one seeks, Anantara Spa is surely the ideal journey's end.

ROOMS
15 spa suites

FEATURES
massages • body treatments • mud wraps • herbal steam therapy • aromatherapy baths • facials • full-service beauty salon • pedicures • manicures • spa cuisine • yoga

NEARBY
Commune by the Great Wall Kempinski • Great Wall

CONTACT
Commune by the Great Wall Kempinski, The Great Wall Exit at Shuiguan, Badaling Highway, Beijing 100022 • telephone: +86.10.8118 1888 ext 5100, 5101 • facsimile: +86.10.8118 1522 • email: anantaraspa@commune.com.cn • website: www.anantaraspa.com

index

index

index

picturecredits+acknowledgements

The publisher would like to thank the following for permission to reproduce their photographs:

Adrian Bradshaw/epa/Corbis 62
AFP/AFP/Getty Images 25
Anantara Spa 194–195
Ascott Beijing 70–73
Bayhood No. 9 74–75
Bettmann/Corbis 14 (top)
blue jean images/Getty Images 68
C Hullmande/Corbis 14 (bottom)
Cancan Chu/Getty Images 30
Centro Bar and Lounge 108–109
CHI, The Spa 176–177
Chien Min Chung/OnAsia 64 (top)
China Photos/Getty Images 5, 13 (top), 37, 38 (bottom), 39, 40, 65, 132, 145, 168 (bottom), 183
China World Hotel 76–77
Commune by the Great Wall Kempinski 192–193
Corbis 15, 20
Cottage Boutique 114–115
Cottage Warehouse 116–117
Danieli's 90–91
Eric Thorkelsson 167 (bottom), 168 (top), 169, 170 (top), 188
Fabian Cevallos/Corbis Sygma 21

Face 92–93
Francois Guillot/AFP/Getty Images 43
Frederic J Brown/AFP/Getty Images 22, 134 (top)
Garden of Delights 152–153
Gideon Mendel/Corbis 69, 164
Gilles Sabrié 23, 26, 32, 34–35, 56–57, 64 (bottom), 140 (top)
Goh Chai Hin/AFP/Getty Images 140 (bottom), 144
Graham Clouston 167 (top)
Grand Hyatt Beijing 146–147
Grant V Faint/Getty Images 2
GREEN T. HOUSE 46–47, 94–95
GREEN T. HOUSE Living 96–97
Guang Niu/Getty Images 27, 41, 67 (bottom), 128 (bottom), 141, 182
Guido Prestigiovanni 28 (top), 45, 50–51, 63 (centre and bottom), 67 (top), 126–127, 128 (top), 134 (bottom), 137, 142 (bottom), 143, 170 (bottom), 172
Hatsune 98–99
House By The Park 48 (bottom), 49 (top), 100–101
Hulton-Deutsch Collection/Corbis 19
Jaan 154–155

Jeff Hutchens/Getty Exclusive 8–9, 13 (bottom), 28 (bottom), 29, 135, 136, 178, 186
Jeff Hutchens/Getty Images 4, 54, 55, 122, 130–131
Jochen Schlenker/Getty Images 173
Jon Hicks/Corbis 189
Jonathan Leijonhufvud and Chang & Biörck 158–159
Jörg Sundermann 44
JTB Photo Communications Inc/Photolibrary 166
Kagen 102–103
Karl Malakunas/OnAsia 31, 60–61
Katharina Hesse/Getty Images 181
Keren Su/Corbis 6
Keren Su/Getty Images 133
Kerry Centre Hotel 78–79
Liu Liqun/Corbis 133
Macduff Everton/Getty Images 171
Martin Puddy/Getty Images 33, 124, 125 (top), 180
Michael Maslan Historic Photographs/Corbis 16–17, 18
My Humble House 48 (top), 49 (bottom), 156–157
Natalie Behring/OnAsia 52, 63 (top), 66, 129
Natalie Behring-Chisholm/Getty Images 125 (bottom)

Panoramic Images/Getty Images 184–185
Park Hyatt Beijing 80–81
Peter Charlesworth/OnAsia 187
Peter Parks/AFP/Getty Images 36, 38 (top)
Raffles Beijing Hotel 148–149
Rechenberg 118–119
Red Gate Gallery 162–163
Richard Nowitz/Getty Images 190–191
Shanghai Tang 160–161
Simon Lim 58–59, 138–139
St Regis Hotel 82–83
St Regis Spa and Club 84–85
STR/AFP/Getty Images 24, 44 (top)
Sygma/Corbis 42
The Dining Room 104–105
The Orchard 106–107
The Peninsula Beijing 150–151
The Shangri-La Hotel 174–175
The World of Suzie Wong 110–113
Torana Gallery 120–121
Toru Yamanaka/AFP/Getty Images 42 (top)
Yang Liu/Corbis 12
Zenspa 86–89
Zoë Jaques 142 (top)

directory

HOTELS

Ascott Beijing (page 70)
108B Jianguo Road
Chaoyang District
Beijing 100022
telephone : +86.10.6567 8100
facsimile : +86.10.6567 8122
email : enquiry.china@the-ascott.com
website : www.the-ascott.com

Bayhood No. 9 (page 74)
9 Anwai Beihu
Chaoyang District
Beijing 100012
telephone : +86.10.6491 9797
facsimile : +86.10.6491 8888
email : info@bayhood9.com
website : www.bayhood9.com

China World Hotel (page 76)
1 Jianguomenwai Avenue
Chaoyang District
Beijing 100004
telephone : +86.10.6505 2266
facsimile : +86.10.6505 0828
email : cwh@shangri-la.com
website : www.shangri-la.com

**Commune by the Great Wall
Kempinski** (page 192)
The Great Wall Exit at Shuiguan
Badaling Highway
Beijing 100022
telephone : +86.10.8118 1888
facsimile : +86.10.8118 1866
email : reservation@commune.com.cn
website : www.commune.com.cn

Grand Hyatt Beijing (page 146)
Beijing Oriental Plaza
1 East Chang'an Avenue
Dongcheng District
Beijing 100738
telephone : +86.10.8518 1234
facsimile : +86.10.8518 0000
email : grandhyattbeijing@hyattintl.com
website : www.beijing.grand.hyatt.com

Kerry Centre Hotel (page 78)
1 Guanghua Road
Chaoyang District
Beijing 100020
telephone : +86.10.6561 8833
facsimile : +86.10.6561 2626
email : hbkc@shangri-la.com
website : www.shangri-la.com

Park Hyatt Beijing (page 80)
2 Jianguomenwai Avenue
Chaoyang District
Beijing 100022
telephone : +86.10.8567 1234
facsimile : +86.10.8567 1000
email : parkhyattbeijing@hyattintl.com
website : beijing.park.hyatt.com

The Peninsula Beijing (page 150)
8 Goldfish Lane
Wangfujing, Dongcheng District
Beijing 100006
telephone : +86.10.8516 2888
facsimile : +86.10.6510 6311
email : pbj@peninsula.com
website : beijing.peninsula.com

Raffles Beijing Hotel (page 148)
33 East Chang'an Avenue
Dongcheng District
Beijing 100004
telephone : +86.10.6526 3388
facsimile : +86.10.8500 4380
email : beijing@raffles.com

The Shangri-La Hotel, Beijing
(page 174)
29 Zizhuyuan Road
Haidian District
Beijing 100089
telephone : +86.10.6841 2211
facsimile : +86.10.6841 8002/3
email : slb@shangri-la.com
website : www.shangri-la.com

St Regis Hotel (page 82)
21 Jianguomenwai Avenue
Chaoyang District
Beijing 100020
telephone : +86.10.6460 6688
facsimile : +86.10.6460 3299
email : stregis.beijing@stregis.com
website : www.stregis.com/beijing

RESTAURANTS

Danieli's (page 90)
St Regis Hotel
21 Jianguomenwai Avenue
Chaoyang District
Beijing 100020
telephone : +86.10.6460 6688
          ext 2441
facsimile : +86.10.6460 3299
email : stregis.beijing@stregis.com
website : www.stregis.com/beijing

The Dining Room (page 104)
Bayhood No. 9
9 Anwai Beihu
Chaoyang District
Beijing 100012
telephone : +86.10.6491 9797
facsimile : +86.10.6491 8888
email : info@bayhood9.com

Face (page 92)
26 East Caoyuan
South Gongti Road
Chaoyang District
Beijing 100020
telephone : +86.10.6551 6788
facsimile : +86.10.6551 6739
email : beijing@facebars.com
website : www.facebars.com

Garden of Delights (page 152)
53 Donganmen Avenue
Dongcheng District
Beijing 100006
telephone : +86.10.5138 5688
facsimile : +86.10.5138 5699
email : info@gardenofdelights.com.cn
website : gardenofdelights.com.cn

GREEN T. HOUSE (page 94)
6 West Gongti Road
Chaoyang District
Beijing 100027
telephone : +86.10.6552 8310/11
facsimile : +86.10.6553 8750
email : reservations@green-t-house.com
website : www.green-t-house.com

GREEN T. HOUSE Living (page 96)
318 Hegezhuang Village
Cuigezhuang Township, Chaoyang District
Beijing 100015
telephone : +86.10.6434 2519 or
          +86.10.8456 6422
email : reservations@green-t-house.com
website : www.green-t-house.com

Hatsune (page 98)
Heqiao Group Building C #201
8A Guanghua Road
Chaoyang District
Beijing 100026
telephone : +86.10.6581 3939
facsimile : +86.10.6583 2133
email : hatsunesushi@yahoo.com

House By The Park (page 100)
2/F Club House
Block 19, China Central Place
89 Jianguo Road
Chaoyang District
Beijing 100025
telephone : +86.10.6530 7770
facsimile : +86.10.6530 7771
email : housebythepark@tunglok.com
website : tunglok.com/housebythepark

Jaan (page 154)
Raffles Beijing Hotel
33 East Chang'an Avenue
Dongcheng District
Beijing 100004
telephone : +86.10.6526 3388
facsimile : +86.10.8500 4380
email : beijing@raffles.com
website : www.beijing.raffles.com

Kagen (page 102)
Heqiao Group Building B1
8A Guanghua Road
Chaoyang District
Beijing 100026
telephone : +86.10.6581 3939
facsimile : +86.10.6583 2133
email : hatsunesushi@yahoo.com

My Humble House (page 156)
Beijing Oriental Plaza
Podium Level W3 #01-07, Office Towers
1 East Chang'an Avenue
Dongcheng District
Beijing 100738
telephone : +86.10.8518 8811
facsimile : +86.10.8518 6249
email : mhh@tunglok.com
website : www.tunglok.com

The Orchard (page 106)
Hegezhuang Village
Cuigezhuang Township, Chaoyang District
Beijing 100103
telephone : +86.139.1121 1965
email : theorchardbj@yahoo.com

SPAS

Anantara Spa (page 194)
Commune by the Great Wall Kempinski
The Great Wall Exit at Shuiguan
Badaling Highway
Beijing 100022
telephone : +86.10.8118 1888
          ext 5100, 5101
facsimile : +86.10.8118 1522
email : anantaraspa@commune.com.cn
website : www.anataraspa.com

CHI, The Spa (page 176)
The Shangri-La Hotel, Beijing
29 Zizhuyuan Road
Haidian District
Beijing 100089
telephone : +86.10.6841 2211
facsimile : +86.10.6841 8002/3
email : slb@shangri-la.com
website : www.shangri-la.com

St Regis Spa & Club (page 84)
St Regis Hotel
21 Jianguomenwai Avenue
Chaoyang District
Beijing 100020
telephone : +86.10.6460 6688
facsimile : +86.10.6460 3299
email : stregis.beijing@stregis.com
website : www.stregis.com/beijing

Zenspa (page 86)
House 1
8A Xiaowuji Road
Chaoyang District
Beijing 1000023
telephone : +86.10.8731 2530
facsimile : +86.10.8731 2539
email : info@zenspa.com.cn
website : www.zenspa.com.cn

SHOPS

Chang & Biörck (page 158)
Sky & Sea Business Plaza
Building A
Suite 511
107 North Dongsi Avenue
Dongcheng District
Beijing 100007
telephone : +86.10.8400 2296
email : info@changbiorck.com
website : www.changbiorck.com

Cottage Boutique (page 114)
4 North Ritan Road
Chaoyang District
Beijing 100020
telephone : +86.10.8561 1517
email : rebecca0929@yahoo.com

Cottage Warehouse (page 116)
4 North Ritan Road
Chaoyang District
Beijing 100020 (for appointment)
telephone : +86.10.8561 1517
email : rebecca0929@yahoo.com

Rechenberg (page 118)
East Xiyuanxili Street
(yard behind Building 12)
Chaoyang District
Beijing 100027
telephone : +86.10.6463 1788
facsimile : +86.10.6463 3995
email : info@rechenberg.cn
website : www.rechenberg.cn

Shanghai Tang (page 160)
Grand Hyatt Beijing Shop 3 and 5
UG Level
1 East Chang'an Avenue
Dongcheng District
Beijing 100738
telephone : +86.10.8518 0898
facsimile : +86.10.8518 2180
email : contactus@shanghaitang.com
website : www.shanghaitang.com

BARS

Centro Bar & Lounge (page 108)
Kerry Centre Hotel
1 Guanghua Road
Chaoyang District
Beijing 100020
telephone : +86.10.6561 8833
          ext 42
facsimile : +86.10.6561 2626
email : hbkc@shangri-la.com
website : www.shangri-la.com

The World of Suzie Wong (page 110)
1A South Nongzhanguan Road
West Gate
Chaoyang Park
Chaoyang District
Beijing 100026
telephone : +86.10.6593 6049
facsimile : +86.10.6595 5049
email : clubsuziewong@263.net
website : www.suziewong.com.cn

GALLERIES

Red Gate Gallery (page 162)
Dongbianmen Watchtower
Chongwen District
Beijing 100062
telephone : +86.10.6525 1005
facsimile : +86.10.6432 2624
email : redgategallery@aer.net.cn
website : www.redgategallery.com

Torana Gallery (page 120)
Shop 8
Kempinski Hotel
50 Liangmaheqiao Road
Chaoyang District
Beijing 100016
telephone : +86.10.6465 3388
          ext 5542
facsimile : +86.10.6465 3366
email : gallery@toranahouse.com
website : www.toranahouse.com